Prepare For Take Off

By
Rick McNeely

A Publication of Christ To The World Ministries

PREPARE FOR TAKE OFF
by Rick McNeely

ISBN: 978-09828655-0-7

Cover design: Jonathan McNeely
Layout & Formatting: Glynn M. Davis
Editing & Proofing: Susan Morris
Eagle Photos courtesy of: Jay Turner@Shiloh Eagles.com

Published for **Rick McNeely, Christ To The World Ministries** by:
Jostens Commercial Publications
401 Science Park Road
State College, PA 16803
Mike McCoy
mccoym@uplink.net
www.jostens.com
Toll-free (878) 897-9693
Fax (717) 935-2283

Printed in the United States of America
Published September 2011

Dedicated to

*My wonderful wife Debbie, whose beauty
radiates from within and without.*

*Without her encouragement, this book
would never have become a reality.*

*Heaven smiled upon me the day
you entered my life.*

*You are indeed the best gift God
has ever given me, and I love
you with all my Heart.*

In Loving Memory Of

Delbert McNeely   Pauline McNeely
1929-1976   1934-2008

My Dad and Mom

*Words can never express how grateful
I am to be your son.*

*God's gift of memories is like a
refreshing spring rain.*

When I feel dry, I remember.

Special Thanks

To My Pastors Don and Deborah Russell,

who have faithfully poured into me for the last thirty years of
my life and allowed me to marry their beautiful daughter.
Thank you for watching for my soul and
loving me like a son.

To Pastor Glynn Davis

For all the years of encouragement. You have been a friend indeed.
Thank you for all the long hours of getting this manuscript in book
form. I am blessed to call you friend.

To Susan Morris

For all the long hours you spent making sure I was grammatically
correct with every t crossed and every i dotted. I felt like I was in
school again, thanks for being a patient teacher.

To Bethany and Jonathan

When God gave your mother and I the two of you, He made all our
dreams come true. Being your Father has been one of the greatest high-
lights of my life.
I love you both more than words can express

To Landon and Shalee

For helping me understand the Grand in Grandchildren.
May the stars always twinkle in your world, for you both made them
twinkle in mine.

To Adam

Every young lady dreams of the day some young man will sweep her
off her feet and she falls into his arms. I am thankful when our daughter fell, it was your arms that caught her.

To Rachel

There comes a time in a young man's life that he must find the
young lady God has prepared for him, until he does he feels incomplete.
Our son's search for that special some one ended when he found you.
Welcome to our family, we are so glad you're here.

PREPARE FOR TAKE OFF

Table Of Contents

Foreward - Bishop Randy Clark

Foreward -Pastor Glynn M. Davis

Preface -Rick McNeely

Introduction - Rick McNeely

PREPARE FOR TAKE OFF

Foreward
By Bishop Randy Clark

Rick McNeely is a man of extraordinary faith in God and compassion for hurting people. He not only carries a powerful anointing to preach the Gospel but also possesses an extraordinary ability to create solutions and to rally people for a cause. He always finds a way to help regardless of the need or what it takes to meet it.

I have listened to Rick preach many times and always found that his messages are filled with hope and real life answers. He has a unique way of opening the scripture and applying them to all of us. His messages are clear and relevant and touch the deepest part of my being. "Prepare For Takeoff" is a must read for everyone. It was a pleasure to read and hard to put down. The real life stories about his family and friends reveal his true heart and the wisdom God has given him. The unique fashion in which he explained portions of the Bible are eye opening and revelatory.

His book will expand your thinking and cause you to realize the power of God's love and His desire to elevate your life. I am certain that you will enjoy this great book and want to hear more of what God is saying through Rick McNeely.

Bishop Randy Clark
Triumph Church
Nederland, Texas, Beaumont, Texas, Sugarland, Texas

Foreward
By Pastor Glynn M. Davis

We met Rick and Debbie McNeely in 1985 and knew immediately that they were special people in the Kingdom of God. Far too seldom do you find both incredible gifts and strong integrity in the same person, but you find that in Evangelist Rick McNeely. We have been friends from day one and we are still one of his biggest fans.

We have traveled on overseas missions together, vacationed in the great Rocky Mountains, spent a week watching Christmas movies in Galveston, (we are both fans of Christmas movies), and he and Debbie are our favorite evangelist. We have been able to watch their children grow up to have great ministries of their own.

Rick McNeely's impact on our lives, and the members of Abundant Life Church, as well as hundreds of other churches around the world, can only be measured by eternity. He is an amazing preacher and God has blessed him with a great anointing. He is an encourager and has touched the hearts of thousands of hurting people with the restoring Word of God. He is one of the few preachers I know who can minister to children, teens, and adults with great grace.

His compassion for hurting people challenges us all, and those of us who have been privileged to be around Rick McNeely, are the better for it! He is a man of faith and action and has a gift in bringing people together for a common cause.

He and Debbie are founders and directors of "Christ To The World Ministry". From America to Africa, from Russia to South America, from Haiti to Mexico and Trinidad, you will find them building churches, feeding the hungry, responding to natural disasters, and training pastors.

We are so excited about "Prepare For Take Off." This is a powerful book that will bless and touch your life in a wonderful way. This book truly is the heart of Rick McNeely, and you can't read "Prepare For Take Off" without feeling the wind under your own wings propelling you into your own blessed destiny.

Glynn & Carolyn Davis
Senior Pastors, Abundant Life Church
Garland, Texas

Get Ready To Fly

I am writing this book with one goal in mind--to help us better understand how God feels about us and how He wants to relate to us. If our perception of God becomes tainted, it can adversely affect our entire life. In the Garden of Eden, the serpent managed to altar Eve's perception of God and it led to the sin of disobedience. Then, sin led Adam and Eve to hide from the presence of God, and we have been doing the same thing ever since.

What do I mean? Like Adam and Eve, we have a hard time believing that God could still love us after we have failed. That does not mean we think He does not care about us. It's just that we are of the opinion that He likes to keep His distance. An occasional pat on the head is what we expect and even an embrace now and then, but to think that God could still want an intimate relationship with us is just unimaginable. After all, look at what we have done. We have failed, sinned, fallen short and now our guilt keeps us hiding from His presence. We are too ashamed to face Him. Thank goodness we don't have to confess what we have been thinking, or we wouldn't be able to look anyone in the face. But that's the whole point, we do have to confess. While the scripture tells us to confess our faults one to another, does that mean we are to air all our dirty laundry? Of course not, but it does mean that we must acknowledge not only to God, but also to ourselves and each other that we are sinners in need of a savior. If we want forgiveness, we must also be willing to give it, but it's hard to forgive others when we find it so difficult to forgive ourselves. The dilemma we face is believing that a God that knows all there is to know about us would still want anything to do with us. We want to receive His forgiveness, but struggle with accepting it. Forgiveness and acceptance work like the hinges on a door--to have one without the other leaves us hanging unbalanced and awkward, but when they come together, not only does the door open, but a brand new life emerges. It is just hard for us to imagine that He really loves us as his own. And yet we belong to him, purchased with His blood. The truth is God loves us so much He would rather die for us than live without us.

For God so loved the world, that He gave his only-

begotten Son, that whosoever believeth in Him
should not perish, but have everlasting life.

(John 3:16, KJV)

He was willing to give His son so that we might become sons. My prayer is that this book will allow you to stop seeing yourself through the eyes of man and begin to see yourself through the eyes of God. I am convinced that then you will understand how He really feels about you. As much as you want a relationship with Him, He desires one with you even more. God uses those things that He has created to speak to us of life and love. If we have a question concerning resourcefulness or laziness, the scripture tells us:

Go to the ant, thou sluggard; consider her ways,
and be wise -**(Prov. 6:6 KJV)**

If we have a question about God's existence we find the answer in the book of Psalms:

How clearly the sky reveals God's glory! How plainly it shows what he has done! Each day announces it to the following day; each night repeats it to the next.

No speech or words are used, no sound is heard;
yet their message goes out to all the world and is
heard to the ends of the earth. **(Psalms 19:1-4 GNB)**

And, if we have a question about God's care and love for
us, look to the eagle:

And Moses went up to God, and the LORD called to
him from the mountain, saying, "Thus you shall
say to the house of Jacob, and tell the children of
Israel "You have seen what I did to the Egyptians,
and how I bore you on eagles" wings and brought
you to Myself. Now therefore, if you will indeed
obey My voice and keep My covenant, then you
shall be a special treasure to Me above all people;
for all the earth is Mine.

(Exod 19:3-5 NKJV)

In scripture, God refers to himself as an eagle. This is not
by chance. There are characteristics about the eagle and
the relationship it has with its young that are a parallel to
the type of relationship God wants to have with us. After
all, who would know the bird better than the one who created it? As we explore the life of an eagle, we will begin to

discover the type of relationship God wants with us. So spread your wings and get ready to fly as you prepare for takeoff!

Rick McNeely

Founder/Director

Christ To The World Ministry
Morley, Missouri

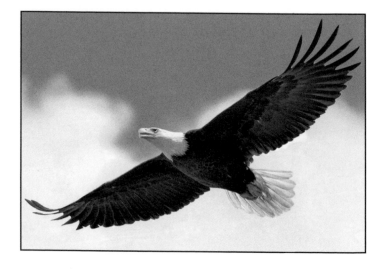

Introduction

Any pilot will tell you that before an aircraft can take off there are many preflight checks that must occur. Each is critical if the aircraft is going to be successfully launched. So it is with our faith. We desire to be all we can be for God. We visualize ourselves flying off into the wild blue yonder, but when it comes time to spread our wings, we feel grounded. The guilt of yesterday is too heavy to lift.

Promises that were made and never kept, keep us tied to the tarmac of life. A Bitter and broken spirit is like a strong head wind we cannot push past. This book will help with the check list. It isn't that we can't fly, we just need to get rid of some of the extra weight. Remember the writer of Hebrews cautions us, ".... *let us lay aside every weight, and the sin which doth so easily beset us...,*"**(Heb. 12:1)**.

Every weight isn't necessarily a sin, but it has the same effect, crash and burn. All of these things can be overcome, if we are willing to deal with them. To ignore a rattle in the engine is not to anyone's benefit. The preflight check list has been prepared by professionals that want your flight to be safe and sustainable. There is a reason it is called a pre-flight check list, these are the things that must be checked before we fly. The list is not intended to be scrutinized during our flight, they must be dealt with before we spread our wings. Believe me when I say God desires for us to fly. It brings Him great pleasure to see His children soar, but He does not want to see a flight that ends in a mayday situation. So, please bring your seats forward and place your tray tables in an upright and locked position as we PREPARE FOR TAKE OFF!

-Rick McNeely

1

Under His Wings

For thus saith the LORD; Behold, he shall fly   as an eagle,and shall spread his wings over Moab. **(Jer 48:40 KJV)**

When God refers to himself as a beast of the field, He is the Lion of the Tribe of Judah, king of the beasts; is it any wonder when he takes to the air that He is still King? An eagle's average wingspan ranges from 6 ½ - 8 feet in length. How tall are you?

An eagle spreading his wings for flight would cover your entire body. Jeremiah uses the eagle's wingspan in referring to the futility of trying to escape the grasp of Nebuchadnezzar. But what is this king compared to God? Remember Nebuchadnezzar is the king that grew proud and boasted of the great city of Babylon, which he had built. Ignoring God's warning to humble himself, the king walked into the palace and declared his own glory instead of God's, and immediately a voice sounded out of heaven and declared the kingdom has been taken from you. It happened at once. Nebuchadnezzar was driven out of human company, ate grass like an ox, and was soaked in heaven's dew. His hair grew like the feathers of an eagle and his nails like the claws of a hawk.

> *At the end of the seven years, I, Nebuchadnez-*
> *zar, looked to heaven. I was given my mind*
> *back and I blessed the High God, thanking and*
> *glorifying God, who lives forever. "His sovereign*
> *rule lasts and lasts, his kingdom never declines*
> *and falls."*　　　**(Dan 4:33-34 MSG)**

If we humble ourselves in the hands of God, He will lift us up. But if we exalt ourselves and refuse to acknowledge Him, that very act can destroy us and cause us to come toppling down. Humility or humiliation, trust God or trust yourself--the choice is ours.

I have two grandchildren, Landon, who is seven years old, and Shaelee, who is five. I am sure you will hear more about them later in the book (sorry, I can't help myself), but for now let me tell you about a game that we play with Shaelee. She loves to hide, but she hides in her own way. She will crawl into my lap or snuggle up in my arms, bury her head in my chest, and pretend no one can see her. Forget the fact that she is in plain view; in Shaelee's mind, as long as she is in my arms or her Nanna's arms, no one can find her. I have given some thought to that and concluded she trusts our hands to keep her covered. She is not worried about anyone being able to expose her-- we can even tug on her foot-- but as far as she is concerned, when she's in my arms, she is invisible until she decides to look at me.

Oh, if only we could trust God that way! He would like us to, you know. When we are in his arms, circumstances may tug at us, but they can't overcome us. The enemy uses distractions for one purpose--to take our eyes off of God. Take a closer look at the Word and break it down. The basis for distraction is attraction, and the devil is trying to dis our attraction to God. We must keep our eyes on Christ and ignore the enemy's tugs, which are designed to cause us to

PREPARE FOR TAKE OFF
PREPARE FOR TAKE OFF

fear and doubt. Remember, the devil's ultimate goal is to distract us and get our eyes off God. That's why in a time of trouble we found David looking to God,

I will lift up mine eyes unto the hills, from whence cometh my help. My help cometh from the LORD, which made heaven and earth.
-(Ps 121:1-2 KJV)

David trusted God and found a place to hide under the shadow of his wings, and we can too. Let's go ahead and enjoy our journey, and not walk in the spirit of fear, because our enemy can't even see us. God's got us covered.

Shew thy marvellous lovingkindness, O thou that savest by thy right hand them which put their trust in thee from those that rise up against them. Keep me as the apple of the eye; hide me under the shadow of thy wings.
-(Ps 17:7-8 KJV)

2

CONTRACTS AND COVENANTS

Therefore shall a man leave his father and his mother, and shall cleave unto his wife: and they shall be one flesh.   **-(Gen 2:24 KJV)**

Someone once said marriage is like a screen door with flies on both sides. The flies on the outside want to get inside, and the flies on the inside want to get outside, and neither one knows why. But before we talk about marriage, let's talk about covenants and contracts.

A contract is an agreement in which two parties enter seeking to protect their individual rights. A covenant is an agreement in which an individual gives up his rights to protect the rights of the other party.

My Pastor, Don Russell, who is also my father-in-law, tells the story of when he and his wife Deborah first married; he was nineteen years old and she was fifteen. They had been married for about one month and were living in a luxurious trailer that measured a "whopping" nineteen feet long and six feet wide. Although it was obviously an economy model, they considered it luxurious.. They, like many young newly-weds, were just trying to find a place they could be together and call home. One of their first tests as a married couple happened when Don was trying to install a cook stove for their "love nest," and was busy hooking the line up to their butane tank outside. Unfortunately, he did not realize the stove's orifices were set for natural gas instead of butane, which meant the gas would pass through the stove's burn-ers at a much higher rate than the stove could tolerate. When Don lit the stove, it ignited like a blow torch. He immediately recognized what happened, and he opened the door to run outside and shut the tank off. However, before he could get out the door, Deborah, who was sitting on the bed by the stove, grabbed him by the arm and pulled him back into the trailer. She then jumped off the bed in front of him and shrieked, "Let me outta here, boy!"

Understandably, Don wondered why she reacted that way. The answer was simple--Deborah thought Don was running out of the trailer to save his own skin, and was going to

leave her behind! Why would this teenage girl draw a con-
clusion like that? Because in her mind, their marriage was a
contract, and it was every man for himself. In reality, Don
was running out to save her, not abandon her. However, for
a fifteen-year old newlywed, who had only known her husband for two months before she married him, Don's intent
was hard to grasp. I am proud to say that the nineteen
year-old groom and fifteen year-old bride celebrated their
fifty-fifth wedding anniversary July 1, 2010. Now that's
covenant!

Unfortunately, too many people that get married believe it is
a contract, where each person looks out for their own rights.
Many have the attitude, "I will stay married to them as long
as they make me feel special, like when we were dating."
That expectation is a recipe for divorce. I am not implying a
husband should not attempt to make his wife feel special,
he should; and vice versa. But looking at marriage as a dating game is a mistake, and staying committed to each other
through the storms will become impossible. Remember, in a
covenant marriage, a person protects his spouse and not
himself. A married couple's vows have meaning-- each one
promises to love and cherish in sickness and in health, for
richer or poorer, until death do they part. I want to know

the one I pledged my heart to will not run out on me or give up on me during difficult times. Marriage is covenant and that is what God is all about.

A blood covenant was one that was only entered into when a person was willing to lay down his life to protect the other party. In biblical times, an animal would be split in half, and then the two parties making the covenant would walk between the two halves in the blood of the animal, swearing their commitment to each other and sealing the covenant. God entered into a covenant with Abraham.

Then the LORD said to him, "I am the LORD, who led you out of Ur in Babylonia, to give you this land as your own." But Abram asked, "Sovereign LORD, how can I know that it will be mine?" He answered, "Bring me a cow, a goat, and a ram, each of them three years old, and a dove and a pigeon."

Abram brought the animals to God, cut them in half, and placed the halves opposite each other in two rows; but he did not cut up the birds. Vultures came down on the bodies, but Abram drove them off. When the sun was going down, Abram fell into a

deep sleep, and fear and terror came over Him. When
the sun had set and it was dark, a smoking fire pot
and a flaming torch suddenly appeared and passed
between the pieces of the animals. Then and there
the LORD made a covenant with Abram.

-(Gen. 15:7-12; 17-18 GNB)

What is significant in this passage is that Abraham did not
pass through the blood with God. God passed through
alone.

For when God made promise to Abraham, because
He could swear by no greater, He sware by himself.

-(Heb 6:13 KJV)

For Abraham, circumcision became the part of the covenant
that would signify his commitment to God. In addition, it
was not just to be kept by Abraham, but also by his sons
and their sons throughout their generations, as well as his
male servants. All would be required to be circumcised
because they were a part of his household.

As for me, behold, my covenant is with thee, and thou
shalt be a father of many nations.

(Gen 17:4 KJV)

*This is my covenant, which ye shall keep, between me
and you and thy seed after thee; Every man child
among you shall be circumcised.* **(Gen 17:10 KJV)**

A blood covenant is serious business. Moses would learn
the hard way that breaking it had serious consequences.

*At a camping place on the way to Egypt, the LORD
met Moses and tried to kill him. Then Zipporah, his
wife, took a sharp stone, cut off the foreskin of her
son, and touched Moses' feet with it. Because of the
rite of circumcision she said to Moses, "You are a
husband of blood to me." And so the LORD spared
Moses' life.* - **(Exod 4:24-26 GBN}**

Moses had received a command from God to lead the children of Israel out of Egypt, and a promise that God would
be with him to protect him. Yet he violated the covenant by
not circumcising his son. Consequently, God was going to
kill Moses at the Inn where they were staying, and would
have if his wife had not fulfilled the rite of the circumcision.
Why was this covenant so important? Because it pointed to
the blood covenant that took place at Calvary where Jesus
himself became our husband of blood.

Then the followers of John the Baptist came to Jesus, asking, "Why is it that we and the Pharisees fast often, but your disciples don't fast at all?" Jesus answered, "Do you expect the guests at a wedding party to be sad as long as the bridegroom is with them? Of course not! But the day will come when the bridegroom will be taken away from them, and then they will fast. -**(Matt 9:14-15 GNB)**

This passage of scripture shows Jesus as the bridegroom or soon to be husband. When Zipporah said you are a husband of blood to me, it was a foreshadowing of Calvary. It is at Golgotha that Jesus becomes our husband of blood, and so He enters into a marriage covenant with us.

Marriage is not a contract; it is a covenant. Remember, in a contract each person guards himself, and protects his rights. But, in a covenant a person lays down his rights to guard and protect the rights of the other individual.

Marriage is a blood covenant. In biblical times, after the consummation of the marriage, the bride's father kept the sheets. These sheets were the proof of the bride's virginity, and the blood covenant between the two. Blood covenants could not be dismissed, or slandered. If the husband ever accused his wife of not being a virgin when they were married, the sheets were produced by the bride's father. The elders would examine the sheets and once the covenant was confirmed by the bloody sheets, the man would be beaten and never allowed to divorce his wife. (Deut. 22:13-21) Remember, now husband and wife are one flesh. See the words of Paul concerning marriage.

> *Marriage is not a place to "stand up for your rights. Marriage is a decision to serve the other, whether in bed or out.* **(1 Cor 7:4 GNB)**

The blood covenant that we have in marriage was entered into in the bedroom, but it reaches far beyond it. It is the willingness of a man to lay down his life to defend his bride, a love that does not seek to be self-serving, but carries the other person's feelings in his heart.

Someone may be saying "But Rick, what about me? I gave up my virginity before I ever got married. How can I have a blood covenant now?" First, let me say you are not alone in this situation; unfortunately, many people have given up the precious gift of their virginity because they did not under-

stand the significance of it. Does that mean you cannot
have a covenant marriage? Absolutely not--God wants your
marriage to be built on a blood covenant. Therefore, when
we make Jesus the center of our marriage, his blood seals us
and we become one with him and our spouse.

Now back to the flies on the screen door. God knew that we
would live in a world filled with heartache and heartbreak, a
world that violates covenants and disregards vows, and the
church is not immune to it. As a matter of fact, at the writing of this book, the divorce rate for the church is the same
as that in the secular world. As of March 31, 2008, George
Barna found that 33 percent of all marriages end in divorce.
Sadly, these are the same statistics for those who claim to
be born again. Evangelical born-again believers (those that
believe the word of God as infallible), had a slightly lower
rate at 26 percent. While this is better, it is certainly nothing
to brag about. It would appear that the people who ought
to be setting the example need one set.

The danger we face when we view marriage as a contract is
that we can always break it. The secular view of marriage
today seems to be if it doesn't fit, just walk away from it.
We are not buying a pair of shoes; we are taking a spouse.

Allowing Hollywood to set the standards for marriage is like playing a game of tag with a porcupine--somebody is going to get hurt.

We cry out for intimacy, but at the first sign of discomfort we are ready to abandon the effort. We cannot build a marriage on feelings alone. Our feelings are fickle, and change with the weather. A beautiful day outside brings out the best in us, but let it rain for a week and see how we feel. Marriage is about a commitment to love through change, not a commitment to change our love. So, we need to be sure before we tie the knot we have the right piece of rope.

3
MARRIAGE

An Eagle Keeps The Same Mate It's Entire Life

And Jehovah God said, it is not good, the man being alone. I will make a helper suited to him.
- (Gen 2:18 LITV)

Therefore, a man shall leave his father and his mother, and shall cleave to his wife and they shall become one flesh. **-(Gen 2:24 LITV)**

Marriage was God's idea. Adam did not ask God for a wife. Adam didn't even know the concept of a wife, but God did. God saw that man was missing something. Look at his words. "It is not good for man to be alone." But wait, Adam wasn't alone--he had God, whose nature was above him, and the animals, whose nature was below him, but he had no one who was beside him. So God said, "I will make a helper suited for him." God did not produce another man, but a woman.

Marriage is a sacred institution that was meant to last a lifetime. It is a unique bond between one man and one woman, a union that was meant to be so strong that they would become one. In the Literal Translation of the Bible, it says, "They shall become one flesh." It does not say that they are instantly one flesh, but rather refers to a progression.

Have you ever noticed the longer we're married, the more we are able to anticipate what our spouse is thinking? How many times have we looked at each other and said, "I knew you were going to say that." We can sit at the dinner table and read the minds of one another, and with a certain look, we can transmit telepathic brain waves across the room and seize our spouse's attention. Throw away the cell phones there's no need for them any longer, YOU HAVE BECOME ONE! Maybe that is a bit of a stretch, but you know what I mean, well at least my wife does.

God created Eve from Adam's rib to remain by his side, and designed her to fill the lonely spot in his heart. A man should cherish and protect his wife because God saw that he is not complete without her.

Divorce was not a part of God's plan. Jesus told the Pharisees that Moses gave them a bill of divorce because of the hardness of their hearts, but it was never the intent of God. In a world filled with broken promises, God wants us to know He is not a "love 'em" and "leave 'em God." We will never have to worry about waking up one morning and finding God gone, for He has promised:

...I will never leave you; I will never abandon you.
- (Heb 13:5 GNB)

When one's life has been devastated by a divorce, it is not too late to find the joy and happiness God intended for us to have. But when we go from one marriage to another, hoping that this one will be the right one, we will not find joy. Just ask the woman at the well, as Jesus did. He asked her for a drink of water and His conversation with her that day set her free from the emptiness of the vessel she carried, and filled her heart with rivers of living water.

> *Jesus answered, "Those who drink this water will get thirsty again, But those who drink the water that I will give them will never be thirsty again. The water that I will give them will become in them a spring which will provide Them with life-giving water and give them eternal life." "Sir," the woman said, "give me that water! Then I will never be thirsty again, nor will I have to come here to draw water." "Go and call your husband," Jesus told her, "and come back." "I don't have a husband," she answered. Jesus replied, "You are right when you say you don't have a husband." You have been married to five men, and the man you live with now is not really your husband. You have told me the truth."*
>
> **- (John 4:13-18 GNB)**

> *"The woman then left her waterpot, and went her way into the city, And saith to the men, "Come, see a man, which told me all things that ever I did: is not this the Christ?"* **-(John 4:28-29 KJV)**

In the midst of everything else that is in this story, there is an important point I want to emphasize. When Jesus told the woman to go get her husband, He was not setting her up to embarrass her. He already knew her story, but He wanted her to know He had the power to rewrite it. It did not have to end with five ex-husbands and shacking up. Jesus wanted to write a new ending for her; after all, He is the author and the finisher of our faith! When He said, "Go call your husband and come back," He was saying, "It's time to get your life on the right track and you can't do it if you're on the wrong train." The words of Christ are words of hope. When He called the man her husband, He was saying, "This can be the first day of the rest of your life--

"Old things are passed away, behold all things have become new" -(**2 Cor 5:17 NKJV**).

Jesus desired for the woman at the well to have a new life, but in order for that to happen she needed to acknowledge the old life was wrong. When He instructed her to go and bring back the man she had been living with, He was telling her it was time to set some things straight, and it should start at home.

No more living together--this marriage was going to be different from the rest, because God was going to be in the middle of it.

In the Garden of Eden, God and man walked together. God saw in order for man to be complete, He needed to add a woman. Now we must see that for a marriage to be complete, we must add God. I am not speaking of only attending church; I am talking about a relationship that helps us become one with God and each other. "Lord, make them one as we are one," was Jesus' prayer in the garden for His disciples. Not only do we need to spend time with God as individuals, but we also need to spend time with Him together, as husband and wife, until we begin to know His heart, understand what He desires for us, and learn to become one with His word.

God made man and woman with a spiritual hunger that only He can satisfy. When He instituted marriage, He helped to ensure we would become one, by creating needs within us intended for the other to satisfy. When we seek to fill these needs outside of God's divine order, it always results in devastation.

Adultery, fornication and homosexuality are just a few of the wrecking balls that seek to destroy the foundation God has given us to build marriage upon.

Sarah honored Abraham, but after God promised him a descendent, blamed herself when they did not have children. When she suggested Abraham have a relationship with her servant Hagar, he should have rejected the idea and affirmed his love for his wife. It was Abraham's responsibility to make sure that Sarah understood God's purpose and promise for their life together as one. Instead, he compromised the unity of their marriage and it caused disunity in their family. God did not sanction this proposal, nor should have Abraham. God insisted upon Sarah being the vessel through which this promise came. As a result, God refused to make Ishmael, Hagar's son, the heir to Abraham's promise. Sarah was Abraham's wife, and they had become one flesh. The promise was to both of them, and not just to one. If God allowed another woman into the picture it could have destroyed their marriage. When Hagar became pregnant, she began to despise Sarah and show her disrespect. Any time we form relationships outside of God's plan it will rob us of peace, thwart our purpose, and obscure our vision. As men, we must make sure our wives feel loved, protected, and secure.

One of the greatest examples in scripture of a husband protecting his wife occurs between Mary and Joseph--they were not yet married, but engaged. A Jewish espousal was the same as being married, except there was a waiting period in which the girl must remain in her father's house. After this period was over, her husband was allowed to take her to his home and consummate the marriage. It was during the time that Mary was in her father's house that the Holy Spirit overshadowed her and she became pregnant. Joseph could have had her stoned, as the law allowed, but instead he decided not to make her a public spectacle. He initially planned to dissolve the marriage privately. Later, of course, an angel of the Lord appeared to him and explained that Mary had not been unfaithful, but was carrying a baby because of her faithfulness. So the prophecy in Isaiah was fulfilled,

... a virgin shall conceive, and bear a son, and

shall call his name Immanuel.

- (Isaiah 7:14 KJV)

When Joseph realized that Mary was innocent of any indiscretion and indeed was blessed among women, he willingly took her as his wife.

Another example of God's intention for marriage to be a lifelong commitment is found in the Old Testament. God told Hosea, a prophet, to marry Gomer, a prostitute. After marrying her, he loved and provided for her, and started a family with her. However, Gomer did not remain faithful. She left Hosea and their children to go back to her old way of living. God then instructed Hosea to find her and buy her back, and take her home and care for her. God was using the prophet to symbolize his love and commitment to Israel. Even though Israel had been unfaithful to God, He refused to be unfaithful to them.

I don't know who betrayed you, broke your heart, or dashed your dreams, but I do know this--it wasn't God. He remains faithful when others do not. God wants our marriage to be a safe place, a place of love and commitment, and it can be, if we keep Him in the center of it.

A Tale of True Love

The autumn air was cool and crisp as John Nordstrom walked into the doctor's office, but the tears that streamed down his face on the ride home were hot and wet.

"How could this be happening to me?" he thought. Things were finally coming together, and all the hard work had paid off. The spring of that year had been a time of great joy, graduating from college the same week his one and only daughter had been born. Now they were a happy family with three boys and the girl they had hoped for. He had just cut his first LP and signed a contract to teach at the same bible college from which he had graduated. Everything was coming up roses, and that was when he felt the thorn.

"Mr. Nordstrom," the doctor said as she looked across the table at him. "The best advice I can give you is to make sure your insurance is paid up, don't have any more children, and make memories with the ones you've got."

John had glomerulonephritis, which is chronic kidney rejection. His kidneys were failing and there was nothing that could be done to save them. The next several months seemed surreal for John and his wife Phyllis. Each day became more meaningful and each holiday more important as this couple sought to make memories for their children. In the midst of watching her husband's health fail, Phyllis's love for him did not. She remained committed to her family and her marriage, praying that somehow God would intervene, never giving up hope, but determined to stay by her husband's side to the very end.

Love's strength cannot be measured when everything around you is going right; but in the winds of adversity, true love stands tall. The world is filled with people who have experienced the pain of being left alone because the winds changed. Everything was fine as long as there was plenty of money, but when the money ran out, so did their spouse.

The promotion at work was what you had been praying for, not the new secretary that came along with it. It wasn't long until the late nights at work turned into a fling in Rio, and now not only is the promotion gone, so is your marriage.

But, for the hurting soul there is hope, and the desperate and despondent can remain confident that there is still one who will never leave or forsake us. God's hands will never let us go, nor will His heart ever abandon us for another; even death cannot separate us from His love.

> *Who then, can separate us from the love of Christ? Can trouble do it, or hardship, or persecution, or hunger, or poverty, or danger, or death? As the scripture says, "For your sake we are in danger of death at all times; we are treated like sheep that are going to be slaughtered." No, in all these things we have complete victory through Him who loved us! -***(Romans 8:35-37 GNB)**

John lay on the verge of death, but he did not face it alone. His wife would not leave him when the going got rough. This type of love far outshines the romantic escapades of Harlequin novels. The love that God intended for us to have and enjoy is the love that can withstand the pressures of life and become more brilliant through every trial and test. The physical and sexual attraction that society is peddling today, seeks only to gratify the flesh, which leaves an individual feeling worthless, with his hopes for happiness laying in the ashes of yet another failed marriage. It is the difference between diamonds and coal--one is cherished and treasured for a lifetime, while the other is burned and consumed for one hot passionate moment that passes along with the night. Which one do you want your marriage to be built upon?

Thankfully, there was a cure found for John's condition. The cure was his mother's kidney. She gave up one of hers so that John could keep living. That kidney lasted for fifteen years. John then found himself in the same predicament, facing death unless someone could come forward with the gift of life, and someone did. His younger brother, Winn, who at the time of the first transplant was too young to be considered, was now ready, willing and able. John's life was spared yet again because someone was willing to sacrifice something very near and dear to him. John's story is not unlike our own, facing death and needing the gift of life.

> *For the wages of sin is death; but the gift of God is eternal life through Jesus Christ our Lord.* **-(Romans 6:23 KJV)**

We too needed someone that was willing to step forward and offer a sacrifice. Thankfully, God was willing to sacrifice someone very near and dear to him so our life could be saved--His Son. What would make God willing to pay such an exorbitant price for us? LOVE--"For God so loved...." -- love is the reason He gave, not because we were worthy or deserving, but because God so loved.

Love is why Jesus became the sacrifice, and he had to give more than a kidney; He gave his life. That's a love we can depend on, and that's the love He offers. Remember an eagle keeps the same mate his entire life and that is exactly how God will keep you!

4
THE SAME NEST

When eagles build a nest, they do not abandon it;
they keep that same nest year after year.
For I am the LORD, I change not . . . -(Mal 3:6 KJV)

A couple that had been married for several years was driving down the road and spotted a young man driving a pickup truck with a girl sitting so close to him you couldn't have gotten a piece of paper between them. When the wife saw them, she became irritated and turned to look at her husband then snapped, "Why don't we do that anymore?" The husband replied, "Honey, I'm in the same seat I've always been in; you're the one that moved."

My brother-in-law James was sent out on a service call to repair a garage door. The address was 169 Mockingbird Lane. When he arrived, he found the side door of the garage propped open with a note taped to it that read, "Come on

in, we will be back in a few minutes." So James went into
the garage and examined the overhead door and found that
the spring was broken. He gathered some tools from his
truck and headed back to the garage to do the repair. He
was about half way through the job when he realized he
needed another tool in the truck.

James has never been the tidiest person in the world, and
on his first trip to gather tools, he was dragging his exten-
sion cord. In the process, the cord knocked the prop out
that was holding the door open and it closed. Ordinarily,
this would not have been a problem, but this door locked
when it closed and needed a key to get in or out. So there
he was, trapped like a rat, (no reflection intended). The
garage door was still broken, and the tool he needed to fix it
was outside in his truck. He waited for the people to come
home, and he waited, and he waited. After about twenty
minutes, he noticed a little doggy door built into the garage
door. He decided Lassie doesn't have anything on him; that
would be his way out! As James was trying to worm his way
through the door, the owners drove up. The man jumped
out of the car with a baseball bat, screaming expletives at
him, while calling the police on his cell phone. James tried
to explain, "I'm just here to fix your garage door, and I saw

the note on the side door so I went in. But I accidentally closed the door and got locked in your garage. I was just. . "

"I didn't call anybody to fix my garage door!" the man screamed. "What? But I have the work order in my truck."

"Don't move or I'll *%*@*."

When the police finally arrived, James explained his story, showed them the work order for house number 169, and discovered he was at the wrong address. The address of this house was 166, but the 6 had come loose and was hanging upside down. When everyone realized what had happened, they all had a good laugh.

While this situation is hard to believe, the truth is it happens every day. How many times in life have you found yourself trying to fix something at the "wrong address"?

You were so sure you could drown your sorrows in a bottle, but the sorrows are still there and you quit counting the bottles a long time ago.

The drug dealer assures you he can fix everything, but the fix didn't fix anything.

He said, "I love you." Forget the part that you barely knew him; he declared his love for you. You thought your knight in white shining armor had finally arrived. But, three months later, he won't return your phone calls. You never dreamed that one night of being held in his arms would lead to this.

"I'm too young to be a mother; my parents will kill me. Where is that phone number? What's that address again?"

And off we go to the place where they said they could take care of everything. It will be quick and easy, and then it can all be forgotten.

It might be quick, but easy, I don't think so. If you think it will be forgotten, try forgetting there's an elephant in the middle of your living room. Your dilemma is you are trying to solve your problems at the "wrong address" with inappropriate solutions. God is right where He has always been, but too often we find ourselves sliding farther and farther away from Him. If we want a close relationship with God, we cannot allow the cares of this life to cause us to drift away from Him. Go ahead; take time right now to slide a little closer. Let Him put his arms around you. You will be

THE SAME NEST

glad that you did.

> *Where is the god who can compare with you-- wiping*
> *the slate clean of guilt, turning a blind eye, a deaf ear,*
> *to the past sins of your purged and precious people?*
> *And compassion is on its way to us. You'll stamp*
> *out our wrongdoing. You'll sink our sins to the bottom*
> *of the ocean.*   **-(Mic 7: 18-19 MSG)**

The good news is we won't ever have to worry about getting this address confused with another, because there is no other like it. And once we make the trip, the way back is easy to remember. Don't worry about forwarding the mail; eagles keep the same nest and so does God. We can always find hope, healing and forgiveness at a place called Calvary.

In case you're wondering if there is room for you in His heart, let me share this with you: not only does an eagle keep the same nest, he adds to that nest every year. In Vermilion, Ohio, an eagle's nest was measured after a storm broke the top out of the tree in which it had been built. The nest was found to be twelve feet deep, eight feet wide, and weighed nearly 4,000 pounds. Just as the eagle's nest keeps getting larger every year, the cross always has room for one more;

though millions have come; there is still room for you. If the cross Jesus carried to Calvary is big enough to save the world (and it is), then it's big enough to take care of you.

So why not take a deep breath and slide back across the seat to get reacquainted. Remember God is in the same seat He has always been in, and we are the ones that drift away.

5
EYE OF THE EAGLE

*I will instruct thee and teach thee in the way
which thou shalt go: I will guide thee with mine
eye.* - (Psa 32:8 KJV)

An eagle has two foveae, or centers of focus, which
allows the bird to see both forward and to the side at
the same time, broadly enhancing its field of vision.
Its eyes are like having a built in set of binoculars. It
can focus on things very close, and also see at a great
distance. As any fisherman knows, fish are counter-
shaded, meaning they are darker on top, which makes
them harder for the human eye to see beneath the
surface of the water from only a short distance. In
contrast, the eye of the eagle can detect a fish under-

water from several hundred feet above. In fact, an eagle's field of vision is so powerful, that while flying at one thousand feet in the air, it has the capacity to spot a mouse within three square miles.

What does an eagle's strong eyesight have to do with us? Have you ever asked the question, "God, do you see what I'm going through down here?" Strong people of faith that we are, we pray for the sick, declare the good news, rebuke the devil, and then wonder if God even sees what we are going through. Not only does He see what we are going through, we can rest assured that He is going to respond to it. He will not let us face it alone. We are the apple of his eye!

He found him out in the wilderness, in an empty, windswept wasteland. He threw his arms around him, lavished attention on him, guarding him as the apple of his eye.

- (Deu 32:10 MSG)

Just as God found Jacob in the above passage, in a wilderness of despair, a windswept wasteland of doubt and unbelief, He may find us that way too, but

He loves us too much to leave us the way He finds us.

There is a story of a little boy passing a pet store and saw a sign in the window, "Puppies for Sale-- $25." When he walked in, he looked at the proprietor, reached into his pocket and pulled out a few crumpled dollars along with some change and said, "Could I take a look at those puppies?" The man smiled and said, "Sure." When he called for the mother, all the puppies followed close behind. Immediately, the boy was drawn to a puppy that was dragging one of his legs. He picked it up and said, "This is the puppy I want."

The owner looked at the young boy and responded, "Son you don't want that puppy, he will never be able to run with you or play fetch. Take one of the other pups instead." But the little boy was persistent, saying, "No, this is the puppy I want; as a matter of fact I've been looking for a puppy like this for a long time." When the man saw that the boy couldn't be persuaded to take one of the other pups, he said, "Well, if that's the one you want, you can just have him."

The owner was shocked when the boy piped up, "This puppy is worth every bit as much as any of the rest of those puppies. Here is $4.75; I will give you a dollar each week until I get him paid for." And with that the little fellow turned to walk away. The owner called to the boy one more time. "Son, are you sure that's the dog you want?" The boy didn't say a word, he just lifted up his pants to reveal a brace strapped to his leg, smiled and walked out the door.

Not only does Jesus see what we are going through, He feels it as well, and will carry us out of it, if we will trust Him.

Our High Priest is not one who cannot feel sympathy for our weaknesses. On the contrary, we have a High Priest who was tempted in every way that we are, but did not sin. - **(Heb 4:15 GNB)**

When my children were young, we used to shut the lights out in the house and play hide and seek. I remember one particular time when I climbed up on the dryer. They walked right by me and never even realized I was there. Haven't we done the same thing with God?

The boss comes and tells you the company has decided to do some cutting back and they are doing away with your job.

You have your face pressed against the nursery window looking at all the newborn babies trying to find yours when the doctor walks in to say, "There were some complications with the delivery."

It's your anniversary, but your dreams of a big night out turn into a nightmare when you discover he walked out. And now, on a tear stained pillow you cry out, "God where are you?"

He is there in all these instances; we may not be able to see him, but He can see us and He loves us. David was so confident of God's eyes upon his life he wrote:

If I ascend up into heaven, thou art there: if I make my bed in hell, behold, thou art there.
- **(Psa 139:8 KJV)**

David knew God was with us in the good times and the bad, always watching over us, when we feel him, and even when we don't. God's name is not even mentioned in the book of Esther, but that does not mean He is not there. Remember her story?

Her people were marked for slaughter with no hope in sight. But, just because they couldn't see God doesn't mean He wasn't there. Who caused a foreigner taken into captivity to become queen of the land?

Who robbed the king of his sleep the night before Mordecai was to be hanged? And who turned everything around and gave them victory in the midst of defeat?

God sees us at all times, even when we feel like He doesn't. There are times we may ask, why doesn't He stop all this pain? The answer is love cannot be measured by keeping us from trouble and hurt, but rather by seeing us through it. How many of us as parents bought our children bicycles, knowing that in the process of learning to ride they were going to fall and scrape their knees, but we bought the bikes anyway.

Why? Because we knew the joy of the ride would be worth the pain of the fall. God knew it too. Think about it; we are not yet out of the third chapter of Genesis before man falls, and God knew he would, yet He created him anyway. Why? Because the joy of the ride is worth the pain of the fall. Paul says it in good old country boy fashion:

> *For I reckon that the sufferings of this present time are not worthy to be compared with the glory which shall be revealed in us.* -**(Romans 8:18 KJV)**

Another translation says it this way:

> *I am of the opinion that there is no comparison between the pain of this present time and the glory which we will see in the future.* **(BBE)**

God understands that life comes with some skinned knees, and if we are not willing to run the risk of a scrape now and then, we will never fully experience all the joys He has prepared for those that love Him. Someone once said "It is better to have loved and lost than never to have loved at all." My father died when

I was fifteen years old, and the pain and heartbreak I suffered seemed unbearable at the time. I remember saying, "God, I thought you loved me; how could you let this happen?"

I felt as if God had hid his face from me, but later I would discover He was right there with me, even though I couldn't see it at the time. God was not offended at my questions, and He did not walk away from my pain. Instead, He put his arms around me and helped me go through it.

Later in life, I became aware of how blessed I was that I had a father. It may have only been for fifteen years, but He was there. Some 40 percent of children today are being raised with no father in the home. They have never known the joy of playing catch, or going fishing with dad. They have not had the presence of a father to teach them how to be a man and tell them who they are.

You may wonder "Was the love I experienced from my father worth all the sorrow I felt when I lost him?" Yes! Yes! A thousand times yes!

Even though many of us may have had an absentee father, our heavenly Father has always had his eye on us. He cheers for us when we are on the mountain top, and He holds us in His arms as we walk through the valley. We don't have to wonder if He will show up for our ballgame or recital. He is with us on our first date and our wedding day, in good times and in bad, during our joys and sorrows, He comforts, consoles and encourages.   HE IS THERE!

Remember, His eye is always upon us, so let's make sure to keep our eyes on him.

6
SPEED

"Look! An eagle soars, swoops down, spreads its wings over Bozrah. Brave warriors will double up in pain, helpless to fight, like a woman giving birth to a baby." **(Jer 49:22 MSG)**

If an eagle spots prey while soaring, it can tuck its' wings and dive toward it, reaching speeds of up to 200 miles per hour. If you are close enough, the bird may sound like a low flying airplane. One eagle was seen swooping down over a rattlesnake, locking its talons into the snake and taking its head off with its beak without ever missing a beat of its wings.

When I read about the encounter the eagle had with the snake, my mind went to the third chapter of Genesis.

Satan had deceived Eve in the form of a serpent, and it looked as though it was all over for man. But God makes us a promise. The serpent may bruise our heel, but we will bruise his head. This of course was accomplished in Christ; however, it does not end there. If we keep our trust in Jesus, and follow after him, we are told;

> *Everyone has heard about your obedience and this makes me happy for you. I want you to do what is good and to avoid what is evil. the God of peace will quickly crush Satan under your feet. May the good will of our Lord Jesus be with you!*
> - **(Rom 16:19-20, GW)**

What father or mother has not felt their heart race when they heard the cry of their child? My daughter Bethany is twenty-five years old, with two children of her own. When she was two years old, we were at a conference in Indianapolis, Indiana, and she had been playing with some other children on a swinging gate. Do you remember that wonderful piece of playground equipment? It was a gate that had a foot rest made for you to stand on. This was then fastened to a pole on hinges so you could swing around in circles at breakneck speed. The object for the rider was to hang on for dear life, and the object for the one swinging the gate was to try to catapult their friend into orbit. Unfortunately, my daughter stepped into the path of the gate, and found out what it is like to try to stop the space shuttle.

When I heard her cry, something shot through my body that I call the "superman syndrome." It happens when our children's cry transforms us into blazing infernos of passion. Suddenly, mild mannered parents are now faster than a speeding bullet, more powerful than a steaming locomotive, able to leap tall buildings in a single bound. Look, up in the sky, it's a bird, it's a plane, no it's ...., (well you get the picture). Her cry brought me running to her, and thankfully her injuries were only a split lip and a loose tooth, but for me it was so much more. It was my baby crying for help and I had to reach her. As everyone gathered around, they kept cautioning me not to get her blood on my suit, saying "Hold her away from you." But, the last thing I was going to do was keep her at an arm's length from me when she is hurting. I wanted

to hold her and comfort her just as much as she wanted to be held and comforted. Is it possible that it
brings the Father as much joy to rescue his children
as it does the children being rescued?

> *But his answer was: "My grace is all you need, for
> my power is greatest when you are weak." I am
> most happy, then, to be proud of my weaknesses, in
> order to feel the protection of Christ's power over
> me.*   **-(2 Cor 12:9 GNB)**

The comma possesses a tremendous amount of
power, and if not used properly, it may cause a lot of
confusion. Let me illustrate my point. A note was
sent to the pulpit requesting the Pastor ask the con-
gregation for prayer. The note read, "Husband gone
to sea, wife requests prayer." But when the Pastor
read the note, he left the comma out, leading the con-
gregation to hear: "Husband gone to see wife requests
prayer." The entire meaning of the request had
changed. Another case in point was the story of a
lady traveling in Israel when she spotted a diamond
ring she fell in love with. She sent a message to her
husband through Western Union. "I have found the

ring I have been looking for all my life and it's only ten thousand dollars." The message her husband sent back was supposed to say: "NO, PRICE IS TOO MUCH!" Unfortunately for the husband, Western Union left the comma out and the message she received read: "NO PRICE IS TOO MUCH!"

The reason I have shared these stories is to remind you that in the original text of the bible, there was no punctuation. The translators simply placed it where they felt like it best fit. Let's take a look at a passage in Isaiah in the King James Version:

So shall they fear the name of the LORD from the west, and his glory from the rising of the sun. When the enemy shall come in like a flood, the Spirit of the LORD shall lift up a standard against him. - **(Isaiah 59:19 KJV)**

I want you to notice the comma after the word flood. When the enemy shall come in like a flood, the Spirit of the Lord shall lift up a standard against him. The comma is there because the King James translators felt like that is where it best fit. However, if the translators put the comma in a different location, the meaning would be entirely different.

When the enemy comes in, like a flood the Spirit of the Lord shall lift up a standard against him.
- (Isaiah 59:19 KJV)

Like the eagle, God swoops down over the enemy and plucks us out of his hands. The song says "He may not come when you want Him, but He is right on time."

Recently While I was ministering in Louisiana, a young lady came to me at the end of the meeting with a story she had heard on the radio that day about a mother and her son living in Florida. The young boy had gone to the lake behind their house to swim one morning, and while his mother watched from a window in their home, she saw an alligator surface and head toward him. She ran out of the house shouting to her boy, "There's an alligator--get out of the water!" He immediately began to swim frantically toward the shore, but he was no match for the gator's speed. He wasn't far from shore when he felt the jaws of death latch onto his legs. He was helpless, and there was nothing he could do but be dragged back into the water by this beast. But then he felt his mother grab his arms. She had managed to run from the house and reach the lake before the alligator could make off with her son. The battle raged on because the mother loved her son too much to let him go, and the gator's appetite was too fierce to give up a meal. Thankfully, the neighbor spotted what was going on and ran to help. By beating the gator in the head and poking at his eyes with a big stick, he caused the beast to let go. The boy was taken to the hospital to treat his wounds, where a few days later, one of the media outlets came by to interview him. He was asked about the scars that the alligator had left on his legs. With a big smile on his face, he replied, "That's nothing compared to the scars my mom left on my arms." His mother had dug her fingernails deep into her son's arms refusing to let the alligator take her boy, and he wore them proudly as a testimony of her love.

We were also in a struggle caught between the grip of good and evil, one trying to preserve our life, the other trying to take it. Satan was demanding the penalty for sin and trying to drag us off to a devil's hell, and our Father, refusing to let us go. His only desire was for us to be free, and the scars prove it--not our scars, but the scars on Jesus. The soldiers beat him mercilessly, their fists pounding his face until he was unrecognizable.

> *Many will be shocked by him. His appearance will be so disfigured that he won't look like any other man. His looks will be so disfigured that he will hardly look like a human.* **- (Isaiah 52:1 GW)**

The crack of a Roman whip ripped ribbons of flesh from his back. A crown of thorns was beat down on his head, and the seven inch spikes tore through his hands and feet.

> *But He was wounded for our transgressions; He was bruised for our iniquities: the chastisement of our peace as upon him; and with his stripes we are healed.* **-(Isaiah53:5 KJV)**

The scars testify of his love for us. When it seemed it was too late and we were going down for the last time, like a flood sweeping everything away in its path, He showed up to rescue us. Jesus told his disciples,

"No man takes my life from me, I give my life of my own free will, I have the authority to give my life and I have the authority to take my life back again...." - **(John 10:18 GW)**

Who got the last word, oh, Death? Oh, Death, who's afraid of you now? It was sin that made death so frightening and law-code guilt that gave sin its leverage, its destructive power. But now in a single victorious stroke of Life, all three--sin, guilt, death-- are gone, the gift of our Master, Jesus Christ. Thank God! - **(I Cor 15:55-57 MSG)**

7
THE ENEMY

Saul and Jonathan were lovely and pleasant in their lives,
and in their death they were not divided: they were
swifter than eagles, they were stronger than lions.

- (II Samuel 1:23 KJV)

A few years ago, eagles were on the endangered species list.
Not because they were at the bottom of the food chain, but
rather, because they were at the top of the trophy list.
Some hunters wanted an eagle for their very own, oh not as
a pet, but as a relic. They wanted to mount it on their wall,
in full flight, to show off its majesty to all their friends.
Thanks to laws protecting them, the eagle has made a comeback. But that does not mean they are now free from enemies.

Though we are at the top of the food chain, we are also at
the top of a trophy list for another hunter. Jesus warned us

about these hunters, whom He called thieves, and reveals their agenda in the gospel of John:

> *The thief comes to steal and to kill and to destroy.*
> **- (John 10:10 NIV)**

That's it, the sum total of their existence; they come in a variety of forms, but are all commissioned by Satan for one purpose--to take us out before Christ takes us up.

We can learn how to deal with our thieves by learning how the eagle deals with his. One of its enemies is a mite, an insect that is somewhat of a parasite. It gets under the eagle's skin, and left unchecked, can destroy him. The eagle, however, is not the only one that must deal with mites; we have them too, except our mite does not come in the form of an insect, but rather in the shape of people.

Has anyone ever done anything to you that just got under your skin, but rather than deal with it, you just shrugged it off? Finally, in time, bitterness grows in you, and you can't stand to be in the same room with the offender. When his name is mentioned, it leaves a bad taste in your mouth and a sick feeling in the pit of your stomach. What started out as just a small misunderstanding has developed into a putrid, oozing ulcer in your spirit, and it's eating away at you.

Did you know that medical science has discovered that bitterness can cause serious diseases, such as crippling arthritis and cancer? It is by no means the only thing that can cause these sicknesses, but it can cause them. Bitterness is not just a poison to one's spirit, but a deadly toxin to our body. It may seem like it's not a big deal, and it might not be now, but remember, as we have learned in scripture, it's the little foxes that spoil the vine (Song of Solomon 2:15). There is only one cure for bitterness, and that is forgiveness. We must choose to forgive.

In January of 1990, Sue Norton, received a phone call at her home in Arkansas City, Kansas, informing her that her father, Richard Denny and his wife Virginia had been found shot to death in their Oklahoma farmhouse. The killer, Robert Knighton, made off with $17 and an old pickup truck, and had robbed Sue Norton of her precious "Daddy."

The loss of her father broke her heart; she just couldn't understand why anyone would want to harm him. When the trial took place, Sue sat in the courthouse bewildered. As she looked around the room, she saw people consumed with animosity and hate for the man that had murdered her father. They all expected her to feel the same way, but Sue was uncomfortable feeling hatred.

The last night of the trial she couldn't eat or sleep. Sue knew something was wrong, but didn't know what to do. Early the next morning, she had a thought come to her, "Sue, you don't have to hate Robert Knighton; you could forgive him."

The next day as the jury went out for deliberation, Sue got permission to see the prisoner. She remembered, "I was really frightened. This was my first experience in a jail. Robert Knighton was big and tall; He was shackled and had cold, steely eyes."

At first he refused to look at Sue, and when she asked him to turn around he answered, "Why would anyone want to talk to me after what I have done?"

Sue looked at him and answered, "I don't know what to say to you. But I want you to know that I don't hate you. My grandmother always taught me not to use the word hate. She taught me that we are here to love one another. If you are guilty, I forgive you."

Robert thought she was playing games with him. He couldn't understand how she could forgive him for such a terrible crime. Sue said, "I didn't think of him as a killer, I thought of him as a human being."

Many people thought Sue had lost her mind. "How could she forgive the man that murdered her own father?" they asked. People started avoiding her, and those she had thought were her friends would cross the street just to keep from speaking to her.

Sue said, "There is no way to heal and get over the trauma without forgiveness. You must forgive and forget and get on with your life. That is what Jesus would do."

While Robert was on death row in Oklahoma, Sue often wrote and visited occasionally. She said she felt like Robert should never leave prison but did not want him executed. Sue gave an eloquent speech to the parole board, pleading with them to save Robert's life, and many of the members were brought to tears. However, they voted for death, and Robert was executed by the state of Oklahoma on May 27, 2003.

Because of the love and friendship that Sue Norton demonstrated, Robert Knighton became a devout Christian. Sue states she believes that some good has come out of her father's death. "I have been able to witness to many people about Jesus and forgiveness, and helped others to heal. I have brought Robert Knighton and many other men on death row to our Lord Jesus Christ. I live in peace with the Lord!" Don't underestimate the power of forgiveness, for without it, no one can be free.

The other enemy an eagle must contend with is the crow. Crows have been seen flying on the eagles back and pecking their head.

Many of us have experienced it--the devil on our back, attacking our mind. We can be sitting in church when suddenly he strikes, and we wonder where that thought came from. Sometimes we can't believe such a thing even entered our mind. Then the condemnation comes: "And I'm supposed to be saved, ha! Not likely with thoughts like that going through my head." But the key is, when the attack comes, we need to let it pass through and not let it stay.

We may not be able to keep a fly from buzzing around our plate, but we don't have to let it lay eggs in our mashed potatoes (so much for lunch)! It is when we allow the thought to stay that we run into trouble, for a man becomes that which he continually dwells on in his heart.

> *"For as he thinketh in his heart so is he"*
> -**(Prov. 23:7, KJV)**

A thought that passes through the head does not take root in the heart until it is allowed to remain, which is why we must guard our thoughts.

How can we get the Devil off our back and out of our mind? I think we can discover an answer to that by learning how the eagle deals with the crow. When the crow gets on the eagle's back, the eagle begins to fly higher and higher toward the sun, until the altitude and the rays of the sun become too harsh for the crow to endure and he must give up the attack. Not a bad idea--when the Devil gets on our back, we can head for the Son. As we begin to soar toward heaven on the wings of praise, we must keep our eyes on Jesus. Then the journey will become too intense for Satan because our mind is on Christ.   The Devil can't keep his grip on us when we put our trust in God, and because He is Immanuel—God with us--Satan will have to leave us.

Submit yourselves therefore to God. Resist the devil, and he will flee from you.   - **(James 4:7 KJV)**

And the peace of God, which passeth all understanding, shall keep your hearts and minds through Christ Jesus. Finally, brethren, whatsoever things are true, whatsoever things are honest, whatsoever things are just, whatsoever things are pure, whatsoever things are lovely, whatsoever things are of good report; if there be any virtue, and if there be any praise, think on these things.

- **(Phi 4:7-8 KJV)**

When we keep our head filled with these thoughts, our heart will be filled with Christ's presence.

8
LEARNING TO FLY

For thus saith the LORD; Behold, He shall fly as an eagle.
- (Jer. 48:40) KJV

When an eagle builds its nest it makes it in an unusual fashion. The bird will take thorns and place them in the bottom of the nest, and then take the fur of animals it has eaten along with leaves to create a soft bedding to lay on top of the thorns. When the young eaglets reach the stage of their lives when it is time to fly, the eagle will snatch away all the soft bedding revealing the thorns.

Right now all the dads are thinking that sounds like a good idea. As parents, we understand the nest is made to nurture and prepare us for life, not for us to grow so comfortable that we never want to leave. Each one of us has a need to fly, to embrace our purpose in life and discover our destiny, but we can't do that if we spend our entire life in the crib.

Life is filled with stages. There is a time for us to be carried, then we learn to crawl, and finally, we struggle to our feet, wobbly at first and clinging to a finger, we take our first steps. It is a wonderful experience for everyone, but if you are twenty-five and still wobbly and holding on to your mommy's hand to walk, then something is wrong. While most moms are in no hurry for their babies to leave, most dads know they will never fully become a man until they learn to stand on their own two feet.

My mother cried when my oldest brother left home. , He was eighteen years old at the time, her first born, and it was hard for her to let go. My father, on the other hand, did not try to stop him, because He knew Darrell was becoming a man, and He needed to try out his wings.

Do you remember when you were living at home and it began to become uncomfortable for you? You felt like you were too old for your parents to make your decisions, but you were still living under their roof. You wanted to be on your own but you were afraid of the responsibility. You just weren't sure if you could make it, and you were afraid to try.

God did not create any of us to stay in the nest all of our lives; He wants us to fly. I remember when God removed the comfort of my nest. I was a Youth Pastor at the time and holding down a full time job at a local wire plant, and my wife, Debbie, was the church's worship leader. We were also active in the organization in which our church was affiliated, but there was something missing.

While God continued to make his presence known in the services, we would leave church feeling empty; there was unrest in our soul. The thorns of purpose began to prick us and we both knew it was time to spread our wings, but knowing it and doing it can sometimes be worlds apart. It is one thing to have the desire to fly, but it is another to leap off a cliff and commit yourself to it. I have seen men with kites strapped on their back make that running leap off the side of a mountain to glide through the air. I have watched in awe as they soared through the sky, wishing I was out there with them, if I could just skip the part where I have to jump off the cliff.

It has been much the same way in ministry. I saw others out there, and my heart yearned for it as well. But making the leap from the security of a job and comfort of knowing where my paycheck was coming from, for a life of traveling from one place to another, never sure where I would be going, or what I would be getting was not easy. Add to that the responsibility of wanting to make sure my wife and two children were provided for, and you can begin to understand my apprehension of leaping off the side of that cliff.

God knows our anxiety, and that's why He places thorns in the nest. Remember, pain produces change, and even though we may be afraid, when the pain becomes great enough, we will embrace the change. Standing on the edge of a cliff is not easy, but then neither is sleeping in a bed of thorns. That's why God does not leave us to do it alone.

Just as the eagle gives its young a little nudge to the edge of the nest, God nudges us by his spirit. He wants us to fly even more than we desire to. We were created for a purpose, placed in us by God, and He is determined to help us spread our wings.

When Orville and Wilbur dreamed of flying, they knew it would take some time, with a lot of ups and downs before they were able to spread their wings and fly. Though the Wright brothers were not the first to take to the air, they are recognized as building the first successful airplane and making the first controlled, powered, and sustained heavier-than-air human flight.

Though many took to the air before Orville and Wilbur, they could not control where they were going, and they kept falling out of the sky. Going up in a plane with no way to direct the flight and no idea how long it will last was pretty risky; in fact, several people lost their lives doing just that. Consequently, the Wright brothers decided the only way they could take to the air was if they knew their flight could be sustained and controlled. On December 17, 1903, they changed their world when they mounted up with wings like an eagle, at Kitty Hawk, North Carolina.

God wants us to change our world as well, and He does not expect us to jump blindly off a cliff, but rather into his arms. For it is there that we are sustained and find our direction.

> *"Not as though I had already attained, either were already perfect: but I follow after, if that I may apprehend that for which also I am apprehended of Christ Jesus."* - **(Phi 3:12 KJV)**

The phrase "follow after" that Paul used here is from the Greek word "dioko," meaning to run swiftly in order to catch, to be in hot pursuit. Paul was not speaking of a casual walk with God; he is consumed with catching him. Why? To understand the reason he was apprehended. Paul was saying, "I know He has called me for purpose and I am trying to catch the reason I have been caught. I want to grasp why I was grabbed."

The fear of failure keeps many from even trying, but I would rather try and fail than fail to try. If we try and fail, we will live to try again; but, if we fail to try, we will never know what God might have accomplished through our lives. Remember, failure isn't final unless we refuse to get up.

That's why when the eaglet stands at the edge of the nest, he does not stand alone. If the little bird finds itself plummeting to the ground, unable to gain flight, the parent will swoop down to catch him before he hits the ground. In a 200 M.P.H. dive, eagles will catch their offspring on their back and carry them high up into the air to do it all over again. This process will be repeated over and over, until finally the little bird is able to fly.

God doesn't abandon us just because we fail to make our first solo flight--rather, He is there to catch us, and as far as He is concerned, we will never fly solo. He called us and He will keep us.

9
PROVISION

*"You saw what I, the LORD, did to the Egyptians and how
I carried you as an eagle carries her young on her wings,
and brought you here to me. Now, if you will obey me
and keep my covenant, you will be my own people. The
whole earth is mine, but you will be my chosen people,*
- (Exodus 19:4-5-GNB)

Our daughter Bethany was at our house one day with our
two grandchildren, Shalee and Landon, (I told you, you
would be hearing more about them). Somehow, Landon,
who was three at the time, managed to accidentally lock
himself in the bathroom. It wasn't long until Bethany
noticed the handle on the door rattling, and when it continued to rattle, and no one came out, she realized Landon
must be in there. She went to the door and called, "Landon
did you lock yourself in the bathroom?" Landon sheepishly
replied, "Yes."

"Okay Landon, listen to where Mommy is tapping on the door and slide the lock that way," she instructed. "Okay," he said.

Now, I need to stop here and describe the type of lock we have on our bathroom door. It is a sliding lock that latches down. In order to open it, the latch must first be lifted up, and then slid over. Landon was trying to slide the bolt over without first lifting the latch, and could not get out. While Bethany continued to try and guide him through the process, Debbie and I discovered what was happening and stationed ourselves at the door. We were both trying to give our little three-year-old instructions on how to extricate himself from the bathroom. After a period of trying and failing, we could hear him getting a little nervous, and then his voice trembled when he said "Mommy." That was all I could stand--I was going to get our little boy out of that bathroom if I had to break that door down. I called through the door and told Landon to step back from the door and go stand by the bath tub.

Debbie asked, "Rick what are you going to do?" "I'm going to break down this door," I told her. She said, "You can't do that; you might hit Landon."

I called to Landon again, "Landon are you away from the door? Go stand by the bathtub."

Then, Bethany called to him, "Go stand by the bathtub Landon. PaPa is going to get you out. Are you by the bathtub, Landon?" Landon answered, "Yes, I'm by the bathtub Mommy."

"Okay, Landon, I'm going to open the door," I said. I grabbed the door knob with one hand, so I could try and keep it from swinging back, and then I took the palm of my other hand and began to hit the door where the latch was located on the other side.

BAM! BAM! BAM! And Landon was free!

It is hard to explain the feelings I had when I heard my little man on the other side of that door with fear in his voice. One thing was for sure, that door was not going to stay between us. I was ready to take dynamite and blow it off if I had to. Well, yes, I am stretching it a bit, but the point is nothing was going to keep me from him. The passion to rescue has been placed in us by God himself. When someone we love is crying out for help, we do not sit around and ponder what our response should be; rather, we act, because our actions will always speak louder than our words.

I once read a story of grandparents that were with their three-year old grandson at a state park. The child was in their trailer playing at the kitchen table when a mountain lion leaped through an open window and began to attack the boy. The grandfather stood frozen as he looked on. However, grandma immediately leaped to her feet; as pushed past her husband, she grabbed a butcher knife. and repeatedly plunged it into the cat's body, rescuing her grandchild.

If a grandmother would respond that way to save her grandchild, what would the response of an omnipotent God be?

God told Moses to tell Israel, "You saw what I did to the Egyptians." God had used Egypt as a land to multiply his chosen. When Jacob and his people made the journey into Egypt, they were seventy in number, but now they had grown to more than one million. All of their years in Egypt had not been bad ones. During the eighty years that Joseph had ruled as governor, Israel prospered.

It was not until Joseph and all the people who had known him had died that things began to change. A new pharaoh who had no memories of Joseph came to the throne. He robbed the Israelites of their wealth and turned them into slaves. But when they cried out in prayer, God heard them, and prepared to do to Egypt what an eagle does to its enemies.

When an eagle captures its prey, it will carry it to the top of a high rock and tear it to pieces to feed its young. When the rulers refused to let his people go, God reacted in the way an eagle would, and carried the Egyptians to His chopping block. The water turning into blood, the lice, locusts, frogs, and hail, were all the hand of God at work. God had one thing in mind--His children's freedom. Egypt's lack of cooperation did not worry or frustrate God. Because He knew He could hold out longer than the Egyptians could hold up, He just kept ripping away at them. Finally, the people that had refused to let the Israelites go were begging them to leave and giving them all their gold and silver to help them on their way. So, God reminds them in the nineteenth chapter of Exodus, "You saw what I did to the Egyptians."

God not only says He loves us, He demonstrates that love by destroying the door that separates us from Him. That is what Jesus did at Calvary; He broke down the wall of partition and opened the door. The scripture has declared that the wages of sin is death-- it isolates us, and locks us away-- but the gift of God is eternal life.

He is Jehovah Jirah, our provider. God was a provider for Isaac by furnishing a ram for him, and a lamb for us, the Lamb of God that takes away the sin of the world. His provision opened what had been closed.

At once the curtain in the temple was torn in two from top to bottom! The earth shook, and rocks split apart!
- (Matt 27:51 CEV)

A little earlier, I talked about using dynamite; now look at this. The earth is shaking, rocks are exploding, and the veil in the temple that was a locked door to the holy of holies is now not only open, it's completely gone! That should excite us, to think He loves us so much. He refuses to allow anything to stand between us.

A week or so after Landon's ordeal, Bethany said she was at

home giving him a bath, and he was just sitting in the tub real quiet like he was thinking about something. Then he looked up at her and said, "Mommy you member when Pa-pa saved me? Him pushed and him pushed and him knocked down the door, and him saved me! My Pa-Pa strong."

If a little three-year old is able to hold his rescue from a bathroom in such high regard, and honor the one that set him free, how much more should we, who were lost and undone, in a prison of hopelessness and despair, and con-demned to die, honor the God that rescued us,?   In the words of my grandson, "My Abba Strong."

God not only ripped the Egyptians apart, He gave their spoils to His children.

> *The LORD made the Egyptians respect the people and give them what they asked for. In this way the Israelites carried away the wealth of the Egyptians.*
> - **(Exodus 12:36 GNB)**

When God's people left Egypt, the bible says they left with a "high hand," which means to exalt in power. They had spent four-hundred years laboring and toiling as slaves on this land. Even though the Egyptians despised them and showed them no respect, they were not whipped and defeated when God brought them out. He brought them out in power. They were respected and feared; the wealth of the wicked had indeed been laid up for the righteous.

"Wherefore criest thou unto me? Speak unto the children of Israel, that they go forward . . ."

- **(Exodus 14:15 KJV)**

God didn't bring the Israelites out to give them up. The hounds of hell had been kept at bay, and even though there was a sea in front of them, and an army behind them, He would be with them! God seemed to be saying, "No obstacle is too big for me to overcome."

You have never had a problem that caused God to wring His hands and pace heaven's floor wondering what to do. He simply spreads His wings and calls to us,

". . . all ye that are weary and heavy laden come unto me and I will give you rest." -**(Matthew 11:28 KJV)**

We are invited to mount up with wings like an eagle. The Red sea became a way of escape for Israel and a watery grave for the Egyptians. We don't have to worry about our past following us, for the one that called us out is able to bear us up.

10

ON EAGLES WINGS

The LORD was like an eagle teaching its young to fly,
always ready to swoop down and catch them on its back.
- (Deu 32:11 CEV)

My little granddaughter Shalee is now enjoying a tradition that began with my grandson. I pick her up and glide her through the air singing, "She flies through the air with the greatest of ease, the little young girl on the flying trapeze." The truth be told, when she first experienced this little ritual, I'm not sure she liked it. She seemed a little apprehensive at first, but now, not only does she smile and wrinkle her nose, she comes looking for more. She will lean out of her mother's arms toward me, desiring one more flight. If her momma lets her down on the floor, she will come scurrying across the floor with her arms extended and I know that means, "I want to fly again." And so once again we take to the air, with her not gripping my arms or my hands tightly, but rather waving her hands in the air, throwing her head back and laughing--that's right, she laughs. You may wonder how she could laugh when she is being jostled back and forth in my arms like a rag doll. The answer is quite simple--she is enjoying the ride. How about you, are you enjoying yours?

An eagle does not carry its young in its talons, as most birds do, but rather carries them on its back. It is relaying a message to all the archers below-- before you get to my children, you must go through me. In the book of Job, God speaks to Job concerning a sea monster, called Leviathan. God asks the question,

> *Can you draw out Leviathan with a hook? Will you play with him as a bird? Can you fill his skin with harpoons, or his head with fishing spears? No one is so fierce that would dare stir him up. Who then is able to stand against Me?* - **(Job 41 NKJV)**

God wants us to understand that while we do not have the strength to overcome the enemy alone, the enemy does not have the strength to overcome God at all, and it is God who fights for us. His desire is not only for us to live for Him, but to enjoy our journey. If we are constantly living in fear of the Devil or have doubts about our future, then we have not placed our trust in Him.

Do you remember when you were just a child, and your Dad said we are going on vacation? As you traveled to that new destination, did you sit in the car and worry about being lost? I doubt it. Did you worry that there might not be enough gas in the tank to make the trip? (Are you kidding me?) Did you lose sleep the night before wondering if the right amount of air pressure was in the tires? Of course not; you played games in the car, took in the scenery, thought about all the fun you were going to have when you finally arrived, and you left the cares of the trip to the man sitting behind the wheel.

Who is sitting behind the steering wheel of our lives? God wants to be, and if we will let him, then we can enjoy our journey, too.

Perhaps you are saying, "Now wait a minute Rick, this is no vacation I'm on." Well, maybe it should be. Let's take a look at the word--the base word for vacation is vacate, which means to make vacant. The word vacant means to be free, unencumbered by business or care. Isn't it time for us to vacate our worries and fears, and quit allowing ourselves to be dragged down instead of lifted up?

Casting all your care upon him; for He careth for you.
- (1 Peter 5:7, KJV)

When my son Jonathan was about four years old, we were having dinner at his uncle's house. While we were all in the house visiting, Jonathan had sneaked outside and managed to get up on the swing set and climb out to the middle on the monkey bars. His only dilemma was when he realized what he had gotten himself into he could not get himself out of. I was standing at the kitchen sink when I looked out the window and saw my little boy hanging on for dear life. The look on his face was louder than any words he may have screamed.

Instantly I hit the door and ran toward him, yelling, "Hold on. Son! I'll catch you!"

When I reached him, he didn't need any more prompting; he

just let go and fell into my arms. Not a bad idea. We can do the same; and if you're worried about Him dropping you, don't. He has never allowed any of His children to slip through His hands.

While I was with them, I kept them safe by the power of your name, the name you gave me. I protected them, and not one of them was lost . . . -(**John 17:12 GNB**)

11

STORM STORIES

We are troubled on every side, yet not distressed; We are perplexed, but not in despair; Persecuted, but not forsaken; cast down, but not destroyed;

- (2 C0r 4:8-9 KJV)

He was the Bulldog of Bergen, the pride of New Jersey, and the hope of the Irish. Yes, James J. Braddock was all of these and more, a young man on his way to becoming the light heavyweight champion of the world. Then the storm hit.

In 1929, Braddock had his shot at the title, but the then reigning champ Tommy Loughran took the victory away from him, and three months later the Great Depression took everything else. From a home to a heap, from Wall Street to skid row, and from Madison Square Garden to a back alley, isn't it amazing how we can go from calm to chaos in a

moment? That's how storms generally come, unexpected
and uninvited.

That's the way the tsunami came. Ask the people of Indone-
sia if it was on their Christmas list. Not one person had
written Santa that year asking for a wall of water to come
crashing into their town, with the speed of a jet plane. We
don't wish for them, we don't ask for them, but they come.

Eagles, on the other hand, do know how to deal with the
adversity of a storm. When the sky grows dark, the winds
begin to rage, and claps of thunder can be heard, the eagle
flies into the eye of the storm, locks his wings, and allows
the winds of adversity to catapult it above the storm.

Jet travel has been an eye opening experience. I have flown
in skies of blue for an entire trip only to begin a descent
that led into a storm. It is a bit of information that is worth
remembering, that skies are blue even when it is storming.
Now I know we cannot hop on a jet every time there is a
storm, but we can find a way to rise above it.

That's what Jimmy did; even after he lost his license to box,
he just kept punching, not in the ring but in life. He didn't

quit on life, and because he refused to give up, he was able to get up. On June 14, 1934, Jim Braddock got a chance to fight again against the number two ranked John (Corn) Griffin. When Griffin's opponent was cut unexpectedly, they couldn't find anyone that would take the fight on such short notice, that is, except Jimmy. They decided to let him back in the ring one more time for one last fight. They promoted the match by saying Corn Griffin will attempt to knock out a man that had never been knocked out in a career that spanned 130 fights, 80 professional and 50 amateur. Griffin not only failed to stop Braddock, but became victim to a third round knockout.

Storms don't keep eagles down. Jimmy Braddock ended up soaring to the Madison Square Garden where he would fight not just for a title, but for the expectations of untold Americans who had hung their hopes for a comeback on the aspirations of this one individual that newspaper man Damon Runyon had dubbed The Cinderella Man. On the evening of June 13, 1935, in a fifteen round knock-down drag-out fight, James Braddock defeated Max Baer to claim the heavyweight championship title for himself, and the ability to dream again for millions of men and women just like him.

Facing storms in our lives is never an easy task, and I do not mean to diminish the struggle and the pain involved in it. Yet, if we are to go forward in this life and be all God has intended for us to be, we cannot hide from the storms and run when they arrive. We must be willing to do as the eagle and fly into the face of it. Instead of losing hope in the midst of opposition, we must find a way to allow God to use the very adversity that threatens to destroy us as a wind under our wings, and a resolve in our spirit to rise above it.

During WWII, England was facing very dismal circumstances. France had already fallen into Hitler's hands, and London, the city they loved was soon to be devastated from a continual barrage of German bombing. Hitler seemed set on taking over England even if it meant completely destroying it. Air raids were a recurring nightmare for the British, and many had lost all hope of surviving. But in the midst of this storm stood one man, who not only spoke of surviving, but stirred the hearts of millions as he spoke of victory. That man was William Churchill. The following is an excerpt from one of his best known speeches, delivered on June 18, 1940.

"What General Weygand called the Battle of France is over. I expect that the Battle of Britain is about to begin.

Upon this battle depends the survival of Christian civilization. Upon it depends our own British life, and the long continuity of our institutions and our Empire. The whole fury and might of the enemy must very soon be turned on us. Hitler knows that he will have to break us in this Island or lose the war. If we can stand up to him, all Europe may be free and the life of the world may move forward into broad, sunlit uplands. But if we fail, then the whole world, including the United States, including all that we have known and cared for, will sink into the abyss of a new Dark Age made more sinister, and perhaps more protracted, by the lights of perverted science. Let us therefore brace ourselves to our duties, and so bear ourselves that, if the British Empire and its Commonwealth last for a thousand years, men will still say, this was their finest hour."   - (From Winston Churchill Speech before the House of Commons, "Their Finest Hour," June 18. 1940.)

And indeed it was their finest hour, for though the battle was horrendous and much of the city destroyed, their spirits could not be as long as this man stood ready to pilot their ship. His words brought hope to every soldier's heart, and so they fought on, not for a lost cause but for the victory of every wife, mother, and child of England.

No one knew more about storms than Jesus. The storm that was brewing in Gethsemane makes Katrina look like a drizzle. Hell's hordes were gathering together; their mission was to take out the son of God. How did Jesus deal with the storm? He took it to the Father. His prayers were not self-centered, but He prayed for those that were with him, and those that would come after Him. While He did ask God to let this storm bypass him, He was resolved to face it if He must. And face it He did, not faithlessly, but valiantly. Being forced to march to Golgotha, the place of the skull, He gave his body as a supreme sacrifice. But while He was surrendering his body as a sacrifice, He was delivering ours from devastation. Look at His words,

> *Father, forgive them. They don't know what they're*
> *doing.*   - **(Luke 23:34 GW)**

We can almost hear the wind rustling through the tree tops as He speaks. To ask the Father to forgive them means that He already has. Forgiveness is the freeing force that lifts the weight of bitterness from our heart and breathes life into our spirit. Friday's storm supplied the winds needed for Sunday's resurrection. When it comes to storm stories no one had a better one than Jesus, and He has promised we will not have to face ours alone.

"...for He hath said, 'I will never leave thee, nor forsake thee.' " - **(Heb 13:5)**

12

A TIME TO PRODUCE

There's an opportune time to do things, a right time
for everything on the earth. . .- **(Eccl 3:1 MSG)**

There comes a time in an eagle's life when it will cry out to
its mate (remember an eagle keeps the same mate its entire
life). When that cry is heard, it means one thing--it is time
to reproduce. Eagles reproduce in the air. Their rite of
courtship does not take place in the tree tops or mountain
tops, but high in the sky.

The eagle will meet its mate in the air and lock talons, and
then they begin to free fall toward the earth. However,
before they hit the ground, the bird will spread its majestic
wings and carry its mate back to heaven's heights to begin
the process all over again until the courtship is complete. If
we want our lives to produce for God, we need to learn a

lesson from the eagle--we too must meet Him in the air. It's even a little prophetic:

> *Then we which are alive and remain shall be caught up together with them in the clouds, to meet the Lord in the air: and so shall we ever be with the Lord.*
>
> **- (1 Thess 4:17 KJV)**

I am not saying that we won't have a bad day, nor am I saying that all of our circumstances must be conducive to favorable winds. They won't be, but it is not our circumstances that enable us to take flight, it is our heart.

> *Yea, though I walk through the valley of the shadow of death, I will fear no evil: for thou art with me; thy rod and thy staff they comfort me.* **- (Psalms 23:4 KJV)**

It is not David's circumstances that are favorable in this psalm; it is his heart. Because David has placed his trust in God, it is God that will generate the power of lift. Trust in yourself, and you are left to create your own gale. Trust in Christ and He will produce it for you.

A story was told of the great missionary Hudson Taylor. On

his first missionary trip to China, the winds had died and left them in a very precarious situation. They were drifting toward shore, which would not have been a danger had the shore they were drifting toward not been infested with cannibals. The captain of the ship made a request for the missionary to pray for wind, to which Mr. Taylor replied, "Hoist your sails." Because the captain did not wish to be made a laughing stock in front of his crew, he denied the request. But when the missionary made it known that unless he hoisted his sails he would not pray, the captain agreed. Hudson Taylor had been in his quarters praying for ten or 15 minutes when a knock came on the door. From the other side of the door the captain asked, "Are you still praying for wind?"

When Mr. Taylor responded that he was, the captain called back, "Well stop--we have more wind now than we know what to do with."

Hudson Taylor's desire for the captain to hoist the sails was not due to favorable circumstances but rather to a heart that believed God was going to change their circumstances. In the nineteenth chapter of Exodus, God instructed Moses to remind Israel of how He had saved them. He had also promised them a land that flowed with milk and honey, and in return, they just needed to remain obedient and faithful. God kept his end of the agreement, conquering seven nations and thirty-one kings in the process of giving them the land. But Israel, after experiencing all God's blessings and His hand of protection, turned their back on Him. It was now no longer only a question of their sin, but of their faithfulness. Our faith can lead us back from sin, but sin will not lead us back to faith.

When David was king, his life had not been without sin, but when his sin was pointed out, he was quick to repent, embrace the rebuke, face the consequence, and remain faithful to God. As a result, God loved him, not because he was without sin, but rather, because he was willing to acknowledge it and turn from it.

If our acceptance by God is determined by our being without sin, we would all be in trouble.

For all have sinned and come short of the glory of God.
                              - (Romans 3:23 KJV)

Israel's downfall was not their sin alone; rather, it was their unwillingness to confess their sin and turn from it. Not only did they turn away from God, they embraced idols. However, God was determined to bring them back to Him.

> *Why sayest thou, O Jacob, and speakest, O Israel, My way is hid from the LORD, and my judgment is passed over from my God? Hast thou not known? hast thou not heard, that the everlasting God, the LORD, the Creator of the ends of the earth, fainteth not, neither is weary? There is no searching of his understanding. He giveth power to the faint; and to them that have no might he increaseth strength.* - **(Isaiah 40:27-29, KJV)**

In this passage, Isaiah prophetically foretells the mindset of the Israelites after they have been carried away captive into Babylon. They felt as though God had forgotten them and would never look their way again. However, God never intended to destroy Israel in their captivity, but rather cause their lives to be productive again. Because He knew they could not produce wallowing in their sin and perversion, He needed to get their eyes back on Him. Only then could they once again be carried back to the heights where they belonged. Finally, their arrogance dissipated like an early morning fog being met by the bright light of a new day. They were no longer confident in their flesh. It is a true saying that sometimes we have to be knocked down to cause us to look up, but look up we must. Where there is faith, no matter how small it may seem, we will find hope, and where there is hope, we will find God.

> *By the rivers of Babylon we sat down; there we wept when we remembered Zion. On the willows nearby we hung up our harps. Those who captured us told us to sing; they told us to entertain them: "Sing us a song about Zion." How can we sing a song to the LORD in a foreign land? May I never be able to play the harp again if I forget you, Jerusalem! May I never be able to sing again if I do not remember you, if I do not think of you as my greatest joy!* - **(Psalm 137:1-6 GNB)**

Israel's captors taunted them by demanding they entertain them by singing a song about Zion, the majestic temple of the Lord whose silhouette could no longer be seen atop of the hill. Not only had they been taken from Jerusalem, but Jerusalem had been taken from them. The city and temple rested in an ash heap of anguish, and smoldering cinders of regret is all that could be found in her now. They learned to cherish that which they had taken for granted, and despise the idolatry that they had once embraced. Odd, isn't it, how sometimes we never realize what we have until it is taken from us. So was their lot. It didn't have to be that way and what they had did not have to end, but regret is the spilled milk of ingratitude. When we learn to be grateful for all that He has done, we find ourselves in a land flowing with milk and honey. However, when we ignore his blessings and flaunt his grace, it will take us to a place we don't want to be, and keep us there longer than we desire to stay.

They had learned their lesson well. The request was met with a simple and straightforward answer--how can we sing of Zion in a strange land? They still loved Zion, but recognized how far they were from her, not because God had sent them into captivity, but rather because their hearts had gone into captivity long before their bodies ever arrived in Babylon. By that time, they had realized their sin, and they did not put on a show, trying to make merry by pretending they had lost nothing. Consequently, their hearts returned home before their bodies did.

May I never be able to play the harp again if I forget you Jerusalem! May I never be able to sing again if I do not remember you, if I do not think of you as my greatest joy!
- (Psalm 137:5-6 GNB)

Physically they were still in Babylon, but their hearts had taken flight. They had heard the cry of their mate, and they knew it was time to produce!

Where has life taken you; has yesterday's promises turned into today's disappointments? If you have never felt regret, experienced failure, or lived to rue the day, then excuse me for one moment as I speak with those of us that have. There is still one who makes promises on which we know we can depend --His name is Jesus.

Let's take a moment right now and let our hearts return home to Him where we belong. It doesn't matter where we have been or, for that matter, where we are right now. The first step is to lift our heart toward the one that is calling our name. Do you hear Him? He hears us; He has seen every disappointment and regret. He has heard us in our anger and our tears, and He is calling. Do you recognize His voice? It means one thing-- it's time to take flight. Lift your hands toward heaven and call His name right now. Let the winds of His love lift you to that place He always intended for you to be, by His side. Lock hold of his hands and let him carry you to heights you have never known. After all, that is where eagles produce.

13

BORN FREE

The captain was impressed. "I paid a huge sum
for my citizenship. How much did it cost you?"
"Nothing," said Paul. "It cost me nothing.
I was free from the day of my birth."

- (Acts 22:28, MSG)

Dust filled the air as a little boy pressed his way through
the crowd to see what all the commotion was about. After
squeezing through the legs of strangers he stood at the
front of a cage and saw two eagles. One was sitting on a
tree limb calm, cool, and collected, but the other had blood
trickling down its head where it had flown into the top of
the cage. His talons were now locked into the root of the
tree and his massive wings were beating the ground stirring
up a cloud of dust. The little boy didn't understand; then he
heard a Los Angeles zoo keeper make the statement, "It's

not hard to tell which of these birds was born in captivity and which one was born free."

The captain had worked and labored hard to obtain his freedom. The very mention of the word conjured thoughts of how much it had cost him. However, Paul was from Tarsus, a land historians believe, though it was not a Roman colony, had been granted freedom by a Roman Emperor. This was the reason for his statement, "It cost me nothing, I was free from the day I was born." Paul's labor had not set him free; it was not his work that had bought his freedom, but the work of another. The voice of an emperor that had the authority to grant kingdom privileges granted the freedom of Tarsus. And since Paul was born there, he was a recipient to that freedom.

The captain and Paul represent a choice we must make. Are we going to try to work our way into heaven, or are we going to accept the King's gift?

Let me see now, I have helped ten old women cross the street today, of which five told me they didn't want to cross, four told me they didn't need my help, and one kicked me in the leg. I wonder if I get extra credit for being wounded in the line of duty. Frustrating isn't it, when we try to work our way into the king's presence. How do we know when we've done enough or even if what we are doing is the right stuff to get us there? How much does our freedom cost anyway? Why not ask the one who paid the price.

The Jews believed that because they were Abraham's children they were free even while they were under Roman Rule, (John 8:33). Great concept; the only problem is they have a birth defect. Jesus sets the record straight: if we are going to trust in the birth process that brings us into the world, but does not save us from it, we will die in our sins. Then, Jesus breathes an eternal truth to Nicodemus under a moon-lit sky: "You must be born again."

> *"How can a grown man be born again?"*
> *Nicodemus asked......* **(John 3:4 - GNB).**

The family name we receive when we are born is not the one that brings everlasting freedom. It is the name we embrace when we are born again that sets the captive free. Think of it, a chance to start all over again. Yesterday's failure can be erased and replaced with the hope a new beginning brings. We no longer have to live in the past, imprisoned by yesterday's failures; we can be free.

Harry Houdini was known as a great escape artist, and he proved it repeatedly to his audiences. Many stories have been told concerning his life and escapes such as the following.

Houdini had vowed that there was no cell that could hold him, and he demonstrated it many times, as local authorities would lock him up, confident their jail would be his undoing, only to have Houdini prove them wrong. One day he was placed in a cell and when the constable closed the door, Harry went to work. A man that was accustomed to freeing himself in a matter of moments broke out in a sweat as he struggled to turn the lock to this cell door. But no matter how hard he tried he could not do it. Finally, frustrated and fatigued, he leaned against the cell door to call for the guard to let him out. When he did the door swung open, and he realized the officer had never turned the key to lock it. Houdini had struggled all that time in a prison that did not hold him captive, in a cell in which he was already free.

Don't we do the same thing, struggling with memories of

yesterday's failures, with sins that have already been washed away? As the scripture declared:

Therefore if the Son shall make you free, you
shall be free indeed.   - **(John 8:36 MJKV)**

The situation we were born into doesn't have to control our life forever; we can be born again. When we become a part of this family, there is no prison that can hold us, and no storm that can keep us down. He has promised to be with us.

What shall we then say to these things? If God
be for us, who can be against us?   - **(Romans 8:31, KJV)**

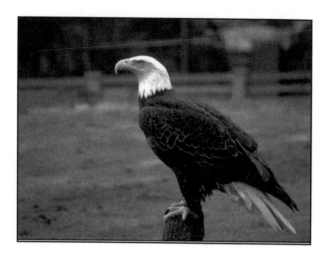

14

THE CHICKEN COOP

And to the woman were given two wings of a great eagle that she might fly into the wilderness, into her place, where she is nourished for a time, and times, and half a time, from the face of the serpent. - **(Rev 12:14 KJV)**

A young man was traveling down a country road when he saw something that amazed him. As he passed by a farm he looked across the field and saw an eagle scratching and pecking at the earth in a pen filled with chickens. The young man was so taken by the sight that he turned the car around and headed toward the pen. As he approached, the farmer that owned the land came out and asked if he could help the young man. The young man replied, "You have an eagle in your chicken pen."

"No young man, that bird may look like an eagle, but he is really a chicken."

"Sir, my life's study has been nature and wildlife, and that bird is an eagle."

"He may look like an eagle to you, but I raised him to be a chicken."

To see that majestic bird in that chicken coop broke the man's heart. So he looked into the farmer's eyes and said. "If you give me an opportunity, I'll prove to you that this bird is still an eagle at heart." The farmer readily agreed, and the young man stepped into the chicken pen, picked up the eagle and said, "You are an eagle not a chicken. You were created to fly through the air, not scratch the earth; now fly into the sky where you belong."

And with that the young man thrust the bird up into the air! But the eagle just fluttered its wings and came right back down into the chicken pen, scratching and pecking. The young man looked at the farmer and said, "Let me try again."

The farmer smiled and replied, "Help yourself, but I told ya that there bird is a chicken."

This time the young man took the eagle and went up into the barn loft and opened the doors and once again said, "You're an eagle, not a chicken. You were created to fly through the air, not scratch the earth. Now fly into the sky where you belong."

Once again the young man thrust the eagle forward into the air. This time the eagle began to flap its wings, but looked down at the chicken pen and flew right back into it, scratching and pecking. The young man looked at the farmer and said, "Can I have one more chance?"

The farmer said, "Sure, but I'm a telling ya that there bird is a chicken. I found that bird when it barely had feathers. A storm had come through and blew down several trees; it got the tree he was nested in. I brought him here and he has been living with the chickens ever since. It's the only life he knows."

The young man looked at the farmer and said, "I'll be back here before sunrise tomorrow and I am going to prove to you this bird is still an eagle; he just doesn't know it yet."

The next morning before the sun was up the young man was

on his way to the farm. As he arrived, the farmer met him with a cup of coffee and said, "I still say you're wasting your time." However, this time the young man gathered the eagle up and left the farm. Together, he and the farmer walked through the woods until they came to the foot of a mountain. Once again, the man held the eagle up close to his mouth and said, "You are an eagle, not a chicken. You were created to fly through the air, not to scratch the earth. Now fly into the sky where you belong."

When the young man thrust the bird into the air toward the mountain, the sun's rays peaked over the top of the summit and glistened in the bird's eyes. Just then, another eagle soared over the mountain top and gave out a cry. The bird the young man had released began to shake and tremble in the air, as he gave out a cry of his own. The eagle then stretched out his majestic wings and took flight to the top of the mountain. The young man turned around looked at the puzzled farmer and said, "He was an eagle all along. He just needed to hear it from someone he could understand."

What about you, are you still scratching around trying to make sense of it all? Feel like you're on the bottom rung of the pecking order. Remember--you are an eagle, not a chicken. Chickens will find a fault in one of their own and peck away at it until they have defrocked their fellow fowl. Chickens scratch and peck, but eagles soar. Have you lost sight of who you are, feel like Jesus could not possibly understand what you're going through? Then you're wrong.

> *We don't have a priest who is out of touch with our reality. He's been through weakness and testing, experienced it all--all but the sin.* **- (Heb. 4:15 MSG)**

I know what you're thinking, but He's God. I can't keep myself from sin; I belong in the chicken coop. If you do, then we all do. There is none of us that can lay claim to being sinless. Jesus alone wears that crown, and as for keeping ourselves from sin, He knows how to take care of that as well.

> *For in that He Himself has suffered, having been tempted, He is able to rescue those who are being tempted.* **- (Heb 2:18 MKJV)**

> *No test or temptation that comes your way is beyond the course of what others have had to face. All you need to remember is that God will never let you down; He'll*

never let you be pushed past your limit; He'll always be there to help you come through it. - **(1 Cor 10:13 MSG)**

The eagle needed someone that understood him and could remind him of his purpose. That's all we need. God never intended for our life to be a barnyard brawl. He wants us to lock our hands and heart with him. We were created to produce for the kingdom and we can't produce on the ground. The purpose that God has for our life is an open door that no one can shut.

Can you hear him calling you? Spread your wings and get ready; the winds of adversity can no longer hold you down. Are you beginning to see yourself the way God sees you? Remember when you look through His eyes you are an eagle, so soar high into the sky where you belong!

15

BIRDS OF A FEATHER

"…..Wherever the body is, there the eagles will be gathered together."   **- (Luke 17:37)**

Jonathan was about thirteen years old when we went on a hunting trip to West Plains, Missouri. Some of our friends had acquired some prime property that had an abundance of white tail deer. We had looked forward to the trip for some time and were both excited, as we loaded up to make the 170 mile journey.

Early the next morning, before the sun was up, we were making our way as quietly as we could into the woods. The year before, we had hunted together from the same stand, but in a different location; this year Jonathan had his mind set on hunting alone. He no longer needed his father with him and he was determined to bag the big buck all by himself. While we were not at the same spot, dear old dad was still close by, not more than a couple of hundred yards away.

Well, the sun came up and after about two hours of seeing no deer, Jonathan decided to start walking through the woods. I guess I should mention the woods we were in were new to us and very thick. I could hear him walking around and I kept thinking, "We aren't going to see anything, if he doesn't stop hiking around out there." That was when I heard him call out, "Dad!" In the midst of his walking around, he had become disoriented and couldn't figure out where he was. I just sat there and didn't say a word; as a matter of fact, I let him call out to me several times without answering him. I was in the woods to hunt and I was not going to give away my position because my son decided to go for a walk. I even thought Jonathan might scare up some deer and steer them in my direction, so I was content to keep quiet and look for the prey. At least that's what I thought, until I heard his call for Dad turn into a cry for "Daddy!"

I can't explain what happened on the inside of me when I

heard the fear in his voice. But I can tell you this, the man that had been sitting by passively listening to a young boy call to him, was gone and replaced by a father standing upright on his feet, calling out, " I'm over here son; Daddy's over here!"

When Jonathan heard me, he called out, "Dad I'm lost!"

"Stay put, son," I said, "and I'll come and get you!" Immediately, I began to walk in the direction of his voice. The problem was, instead of waiting for me to get to him, he tried to find his way to me. Please keep in mind, the woods were very dense. After about ten minutes, he called out to me again, but this time my voice was coming from a completely different location. Suddenly, I heard the shot of a rifle ringing through the forest, a single solitary shot that made my heart drop.

"Jonathan, Jonathan! Son, are you alright? " In my mind, I could see my son tripping over a rock and accidently shooting himself. My heart was pounding and my mind was racing as I listened for his voice. Finally it came.

"Yes Dad, I'm fine," he responded.

"Why did you shoot your gun?" I asked.

"Because it scared me when your voice changed locations and I couldn't figure out where you were," he answered.

"Stay right where you are and just keep talking to me," I instructed.

It wasn't long until our conversation brought us back together again. There is a lesson in this: if we want to stay close, we need to communicate; but more than just chit chatting, we need to speak to the heart.

I wonder what there is in a voice that can cause a parent to go from passive to passionate. You know what I'm talking about. How many times have you heard your children in another room playing, and calling to you, "Mommy, he took my doll."

Her playmate responds, "No I didn't."

Or, "Daddy, she keeps taking the crayon that I want to color with."
And the playmate says, "Nah, I had it first."

We can completely ignore it and let them work it out. But, the first time we hear a real cry, it has our attention!

God is much the same way. If we are going to get anywhere with Him, we have to get real with Him, because nobody knows us better than He does.

> *. . . This people honors Me with their lips, but their heart is far from Me.* - **(Mark 7:6 NKJV)**

> *And you shall love the Lord your God with all your heart, with all your soul, with all your mind, and with all your strength. This is the first commandment.* - **(Mark 12:30 NKJV)**

The day-to-day routine of religion must be replaced with the passion of a relationship that cries out to Abba Father, "Daddy, I want you!" Remember:

> *Wherever the body is, there the eagles will be gathered together.* - **(Luke 17:37 NKJV)**

This scripture in Luke is a reminder to us that wherever Christ is (the body), eagles, (believers will gather around him. Our pursuit of Him must be one of purpose and not just mere chance. In order for our lives to produce, we have to build an intimate relationship with God. It requires trusting in Him and actively waiting on Him. You may wonder what I mean by actively waiting on the Lord. Let me answer that question by first giving you a passage of scripture found in Isaiah.

"But they that wait upon the Lord shall renew
their strength; they shall mount up with wings
as eagles; they shall run, and not be weary; and
they shall walk, and not faint." - **(Isaiah 40:31 KJV)**

While I understand the word "wait" is speaking of looking for, or patiently expecting, it does not mean sluggishly looking, or lazily waiting. Let me ask you a question. If you are expecting visitors at your house, do you sit around all day watching television, while waiting for them to come? If you do, there will certainly be many things left undone upon your guests' arrival. However, if you choose to actively wait, that means that while you are waiting for them you are busy preparing for their arrival. Making sure the dishes are done, the house is swept, the guest room is ready with fresh sheets for the bed; if we wait in this manner, when our guests finally shows up, we are ready to meet them with joy instead of dread.

Now think about that scripture, "They that wait upon the Lord shall renew their strength..," Doesn't it make sense that we will grow stronger in our walk with God that if while we wait on him, we also wait upon him. When I was fifteen years old, I worked in a restaurant as a waiter. After the guests were seated and served, I would pull up a chair and sit down next to their table. When my boss saw me, he motioned for me to come to the kitchen. When I walked back into the kitchen he asked me what I was doing, and I responded, "You hired me to be a waiter, didn't you?" After he answered yes, I said, "Well," I am waiting for them to finish so I can clean off their table." That was my first and last night to work that job. Just kidding, but I actually did work at a restaurant. But my duties were not to pull up a chair and wait for them to finish, but rather to serve, by waiting upon them. I kept their glass filled with water and their cup filled with coffee. I made sure they had everything they needed, and did all I could to make certain they enjoyed themselves while they were there. Consequently, the better I waited upon them, the greater my reward.

Now granted, God does not want, nor desire, our coffee or water, but how about our praise and worship? It is easy to see that the more we wait upon him in these areas of our life, the stronger we will become. When we are obedient to his direction, we indeed mount up with the wings of eagles. Remember obedience is better than sacrifice; just ask King Saul, if we refuse to follow instruction and we're in too much of a hurry to wait upon God, we are going to end up with our wings clipped. On the other hand, if we set our heart toward God, and are quick to obey and give God the praise he deserves, we will "run and not be weary." The giants in our lives will have to take a back seat to the God we love and serve. David was more than a shepherd; he was an eagle.

There is truth to the phrase "birds of a feather flock together." We see it in school, at work, in social gatherings, and even in churches. This is the reason it is so important to safeguard with whom we keep company.

> *Be not deceived: evil communications corrupt good manners.* - **(1 Cor 15:33 KJV)**

An ancient proverb stated, "It is hard to fly like an eagle, when one hangs out with turkeys." I really don't know how old it is or even if it is a proverb, but whoever said it certainly knew what he was talking about!

We have been called to purpose, but we cannot fulfill that purpose unless we fully commit ourselves to God.

> *"So leave the corruption and compromise; leave it for good," says God. "Don't link up with those who will pollute you. I want you all for myself."*
> — (2 Cor 6:17 MSG)

When God chose a people for himself, He called Abraham. However, before Abraham's life could produce, there were some things God required Abraham to leave behind.

> *Now the Lord had said unto Abram, "Get thee out of thy country, and from thy kindred, and from thy father's house, unto a land that I will show thee: And I will make of thee a great nation, and I will bless thee and make thy name great; and thou shalt be a blessing."*
> — (Gen 12:1-2 KJV)

We have become an heir of Abraham's promise through Jesus Christ. And like Abraham, God wants to bless us to be a blessing. But before that can happen, there are some things we must leave behind. He instructed Abraham to get out from his country, his kindred, and his father's house. Let's take a look at these individually and see what they mean to us.

Country

In this passage, "country" represents our environment or our comfort zone. Remember a comfort zone is not always comfortable. It is the reason that women who have husbands who beat them, don't leave. It is not because they are comfortable there; it is because it is what they have become accustomed to. They have grown to expect it and accept it. The country in which Abraham was raised practiced sacrificing their sons and daughters to pagan gods. God wanted Abraham out of that environment, in the same way He wants us to leave ours. We cannot continue to expose ourselves to an atmosphere that rejects God and all that is morally right, without it having an impact on our own lives. Studies have shown that people who are exposed to a constant diet of sex and violence on television will act out that aggression toward others, including their family and friends. Our country does not only consist of where we live, but also what we allow to live in us. Sometimes, in order for our lives to produce, we must seek a change of scenery, not just for our eyes, but for our hearts as well.

Thus, it is time to get out of that old stomping ground and experience a new day in Christ. When Jesus called the twelve, they left everything behind to follow him. They became his entourage; wherever He was, they were not far behind. It was in this environment that they began to grow. He taught them how to love the world without becoming a part of it. He showed them it was possible to rescue the sinner without falling into sin, and He reminds us that no matter what country we were raised in, Calvary can provide a change of address.

Kindred

When God spoke to Abraham about leaving his kindred, it symbolized a way of thinking. When we hear the statement, "they have a kindred spirit," it simply means they think alike. But, if we are going to move forward with God, we must abandon our old way of thinking. When we associate with someone that is always talking negative, it will not be long until we are talking negative as well. When I have spent a few hours with someone that is consistently down in the mouth and cynical of others, I have left them feeling like I need to take a shower! There is literally a residue that I feel on me after being in their presence. That is why Jesus instructs the disciples and tells them,

When you go into a household, greet it. If the household is worthy, let your peace come upon it. But if it is not worthy, let your peace return to you. And whoever will not receive you nor hear your words, when you depart from that house or city, shake off the dust from your feet.
- **(Matt 10:12-14 NKJV)**

One of the underlying messages in this text is that God does not want us to permit anyone or anything to steal our peace from us. Our conversation should always be one that uplifts and blesses. However, if we are not received, we cannot allow it to get into our spirit; but rather, we need to just shake it off and go on our way.   We should not empower anyone to take rule over us with a wrong way of thinking. Young people in universities today are continually subjugated to attacks on their faith by a secular way of thinking or a kindred spirit that exists and thrives on most of our college campuses. Some professors indulge themselves by seeking to disallow any mention of God in their classrooms, unless it is molded and shaped by them. They try and reduce God to a universal consciousness that directs us to hug trees and save whales, never acknowledging Him as the one that created the trees and the whales. They seek to persuade students to abandon the faith they embraced as children and become more enlightened in their way of thinking, rejecting any absolutes like right and wrong, and good and evil. The apostle Paul warned Timothy about this way of thinking:

> *You should know this, Timothy that in the last days there will be very difficult times. For people will love only themselves and their money. They will be boastful and proud, scoffing at God, disobedient to their parents, and ungrateful. They will consider nothing sacred. They will be unloving and unforgiving; they will slander others and have no self-control. They will be cruel and hate what is good. They will betray their friends, be reckless, be puffed up with pride, and love pleasure rather than God. They will act religious, but they will reject the power that could make them godly. Stay away from people like that!*
> *- (2 Tm 3:1-5 NLT)*

The Devil has not changed his strategy--he has just repackaged it. Whether it was Eve in the garden being told, "Eat the fruit and you will be like God," or Jesus hanging on the cross with the crowd yelling, "If you're the Son of God, come down from the cross and save yourself, then we will believe you," Satan's plan has always been the same. He wants to convince you to give up on your purpose, change your way of thinking, lay down your cross and save yourself; after all, nobody else thinks the way you do anymore.

But if I am to stay true to my purpose and see my life produce for God, I must set my eyes on Jesus and say goodbye to my old world view.

> *So here's what I want you to do, God helping you: Take your everyday, ordinary life - your sleeping, eating, going-to-work, and walking-around life - and place it before God as an offering. Embracing what God does for you is the best thing you can do for him. Don't become so well-adjusted to your culture that you fit into it without even thinking. Instead, fix your attention on God. You'll be changed from the inside out. Readily recognize what he wants from you, and quickly respond to it. Unlike the culture around you, always dragging you down to its level of immaturity, God brings the best out of you, and develops well-formed maturity in you.* **(Romans 12:1-2 MSG)**

Father's House

The last thing God instructed Abraham about leaving behind was his father's house. This represents the old, improper relationships that we formed and fashioned while still living in the old neighborhood. These relationships can pose a threat to your new life. Just because you got born again and are on your way to heaven doesn't mean everyone else will be excited about it and want to join the journery. As a matter of fact, not only will there be people who choose not to join you, many of them do not want to see you make the trip either. Some of these old relationships will feel threatened by your new-found life. For them, this born again experience has robbed them of an old friend. They will not be able to understand or accept the fact that you don't want to cruise the bars with them any longer, or partake of the same old entertainment. Don't be surprised if some of them even become jealous of your new-found relationship with Christ.

In David Wilkerson's book, The Cross and the Switchblade, David wrote about how many of the gang's girlfriends would respond when their boyfriends accepted Jesus. When the call was given for those who wanted to ask Christ into their hearts, many of the girls would begin to expose themselves to the boys in a desperate attempt to keep them in their old life style, and sadly, for some, it worked. However, there were those that refused to turn back. Instead, they abandoned their old relationships so they could embrace the new one they found in Jesus. It is important to understand I am not suggesting that when we give our life to Jesus, we should forsake all our old friends. Instead, I am saying that we cannot allow old relationships to keep us from moving forward in our walk with God. And if they begin to drag us down or pull us back, we must leave them behind.

> *All my closest friends are disgusted with me. Those I love have turned against me.* - **(Job 19:19 GW)**

When my brother Darrell gave his heart to the Lord, it meant leaving behind a host of friends that he had built around a life of drinking and drugs. After his conversion, he would try to witness to them. Some came to church with him, but the majority of them refused, or would pretend to be interested, so they could have a good laugh later. They even came to him and said, "Darrell, we will make a deal with you; you go party with us tonight and we will go to church with you on Sunday." Darrell wisely refused. Why? I mean if they promised to go to church on Sunday, wouldn't it be worth it?

> *Therefore, if anyone is in Christ, he is a new creation;*
> *old things have passed away; behold, all things have*
> *become new.*   **- (2 Cor 5:17 NKJV)**

We will never mount up with eagles' wings and see our lives produce if we continue to dabble in an old lifestyle.

> *Jesus said to him, Anyone who starts to plow and*
> *then keeps looking back is of no use for the Kingdom*
> *of God.*   **- (Luke 9:62 GNB)**

God has great things in store for us. But if we are ever to become fruitful, we must, like the eagle, meet him in the air. God desires for us to live on a higher plain. It is here we become all that He has intended for us to be.

Before an eagle can fly he has to get out of the nest. So, say goodbye to your old environment, way of thinking, and relationships. Don't allow them to hold you captive any longer.

We were created with purpose. We have experienced the redeeming power of Christ's cross, and discovered as the apostle Paul did, His grace is sufficient.

Dear children, you belong to God. So you have
won the victory over these people, because the
one who is in you is greater than the one who is
in the world. **- (1 John 4:4 GW)**

I hope you have enjoyed your time with me as much as I have enjoyed my time with you. My prayer is that this book has enriched your understanding of how much God loves and cares for you. It has always been His desire to see you blossom and grow.

I know what I'm doing. I have it all planned out—
plans to take care of you, not abandon you, plans
to give you the future you hope for. When you call
on me, when you come and pray to me, I'll listen.
When you come looking for me, you'll find me,
Yes, when you get serious about finding me and
want it more than anything else, I'll make sure
you won't be disappointed. . .
- (Jer 29:11-14 MSG)

So go ahead, leap out of the nest, spread your wings and feel God's love lift you higher than you've ever been before.

I hope to see you again real soon; until then, may God cause His face to smile upon you and be gracious to you, and maybe I'll catch you on the fly!

References

1. A True Book
   The Bald Eagle
   Patricia Ryon Quiri

2. Wildlife Winners
   The Bald Eagle
   Endangered No More
   Mac Priebe

3. Animal Habitats
   The Eagle in the Mountains
   Shattil/Rozinski/Oxford Scientific Films

4. The Book of Eagles
   Helen Roney Sattler

5. Sierra Club
   Wildlife Library
   Eagles
   Text by Aubrey Lang

6. Eagles
   Lions of the Sky
   Emery & Durga Bernhard

7. Animals.nationalgeographic.com

8. Ohio Outdoor Notebook
   www.ohiodnr.com

9. www.associatedcontent.com

10. www.baldeagleinfo.com

11. Worldwide Laws of Life
    John Marks Templeton

12. Zootorah.blogspot.com

While every effort has been made to site all resources, due to the number of years of collecting information and the stories concerning the eagles, some I am sure have been missed.

Christ To The World Ministry

For speaking engagements or additional copies of this book email us at c2w@cablerocket.com or call 573-262-2326.

Go on a misson trip with Christ To The World

Missionary - Evangelists Rick and Debbie McNeely take several mission trips each year to different countries. Over the past years they have taken literally hundreds into the mission field.

To learn more about these trips visit them online at:

www.christ2theworld.org